THE ROYAL COURT THEATRE IN ASSOCIATION
WITH KANDINSKY THEATRE COMPANY
PRESENTS

More Life

By Lauren Mooney &
James Yeatman

More Life was first performed at the Royal Court Jerwood Theatre
Upstairs on Thursday 6 February 2025.

More Life

By Lauren Mooney & James Yeatman

Cast (in alphabetical order):

Vic **Marc Elliott**
Bridget **Alison Halstead**
Mike **Lewis Mackinnon**
Harry **Tim McMullan**
Ghost Bridget **Danusia Samal**
Davina **Helen Schlesinger**

Director **James Yeatman**
Text & Dramaturgy **Lauren Mooney**
Designer **Shankho Chaudhuri**
Lighting Designer **Ryan Joseph Stafford**
Composer & Co-Sound Designer **Zac Gvi**
Co-Sound Designer **Dan Balfour**
Vocal Music Director **Osnat Schmool**
Production Manager **Zara Drohan**
Costume Supervisor **Isobel Pellow**
Company Manager **Mica Taylor**
Stage Manager **Kirsty MacDiarmid**
Deputy Stage Manager **Grace Hans**
Lighting Supervisor **Lucinda Plummer**
Lighting Programmer **Lizzie Skellett**
Stage Supervisor **Maddy Collins**
Lead Producer **Hannah Lyall**
Executive Producer **Steven Atkinson**

The Royal Court is grateful to Sandra Treagus For ATA Assoc. Ltd for supporting this production. Previously developed with support from Cockayne – Grants for the Arts, Arts Council England, the National Theatre's Generate programme and New Diorama Theatre.

MORE LIFE was developed collaboratively with performers, designers, experts and other artists over several years. Kandinsky Theatre Company would like to thank the company and creative team for all their contributions, as well as Emmanuel Akwafo, Jessie Anand, Afnan Azizi, Dr Paul Azzopardi, Dr Tristan Bekinschtein, Dr Vaughan Bell, Elinor Crawley, Jacopo Crivellaro, Jack Humphrey, Natalie Kimmerling, Sarah Lam, Peter Laycock, Mark Lockyer, Daniel Millar, Tika Mu'tamir, Lydia Nicholas, Dr Tim Nicholson, Gloria Obianyo, Kathrine Payne, Irfan Shamji, Sy Supersad, Danny Webb, Tom Wentworth, Angus Wright and Sargon Yelda.

We would also like to thank the following organisations for their support: Dartington Trust; King Solomon Academy; New Diorama Theatre; RAWD Liverpool; The Royal College of Art; Stephen Joseph Theatre, Scarborough; The Egg at Theatre Royal Bath; and Totnes Caring.

We are grateful for the writing and research of Timothy Carroll, Donna Haraway, Aleks Krotoski, Mark O'Connell, Aaron Parkhurst, Mary Shelley, Robert Sparrow, Émile P. Torres and Jeannette Winterson.

The Royal Court and Stage Management wish to thank the following for their help with this production: Neals Yard, Young Vic, National Theatre Props department.

Lauren Mooney
(Text & Dramaturgy)

Lauren Mooney is a writer, producer and dramaturg. She co-runs award-winning Kandinsky Theatre Company with director James Yeatman. She previously worked for Clean Break, where she co-edited their monologue collection Rebel Voices, and also holds extensive audio drama credits as a writer and script editor for Big Finish.

As writer-dramaturg for Kandinsky:
Mrs Caliban (Theatro Technis / CSSD); SHTF (Schauspielhaus in Vienna); There Is A Light That Never Goes Out (Royal Exchange Manchester); Dinomania, Trap Street (&Schaubühne), The Winston Machine (&Tour inc Marlowe/Bristol Old Vic/Theatre by the Lake), Still III, Dog Show (New Diorama).

As dramaturg: My Mother's Funeral (Paines Plough/UK tour); Fanboy (Pleasance Edinburgh/Soho Theatre); ColLab (LAMDA).

James Yeatman (Director)

James Yeatman is a director, writer and dramaturg. He runs award-winning Kandinsky Theatre Company with Lauren Mooney.

For the Royal Court: The Kid Stays In The Picture [Co-Director and Writer], Posh [Assistant Director].

With Kandinsky, as director and co-writer: Mrs Caliban (Theatro Technis / CSSD); SHTF (Schauspielhaus in Vienna); There Is A Light That Never Goes Out (Royal Exchange Manchester); Dinomania, Trap Street (&Schaubühne), The Winston Machine (&Tour inc Marlowe/Bristol Old Vic/Theatre by the Lake), Still III, Dog Show (New Diorama); Limehouse Nights (Limehouse Town Hall).

As co-director and writer: The Language of Kindness (Shoreditch Town Hall); Beware of Pity (Schaubühne).

As director: Lionboy (Kiln/ Broadway/ International Tour); The Merchant of Venice (LAMDA).

As co-writer/dramaturg: Winter's Tale (Dailes Teatr Latvia); Persuasion (Royal Exchange).

As associate director: Felix's Room (Berliner Ensemble); Grief is the Thing with Feathers (Barbican/St Ann's Warehouse); The Master and Margarita (Barbican/European Tour); Chimerica (West End).

As assistant director: Double Feature (National); A Delicate Balance (Almeida).

Dan Balfour (Co-Sound Designer)

Theatre includes: **The Cherry Orchard (Donmar); Vanya (West End); Dear England (National); Stranger Beasts, I Am Kevin (Wildworks); My English Persian Kitchen (Soho); Make Good, One Of Them Ones, IDYLL (Pentabus); Dear Annie I Hate You (Zoo Playground); Mrs Caliban (Theatre Technic); Wuthering Heights (Royal & Derngate/Tour); Les Dawson Flying High (National Tour); How To Break Out of a Detention Centre (Riverside Studios); Private Peaceful (Nottingham Playhouse/ Tour); Two Character Play, Wilderness (Hampstead); The Hatchling (Trigger Productions); hang (Sheffield Crucible); Counting Sheep (Belarus Free Theatre); Sugar Syndrome, The Misfortune Of The English (Orange Tree); Operation Mincemeat (New Diorama); Effigies of Wickedness (Gate); Great Apes, Sputnik Sweetheart, Dance Of Death (Arcola).**

Film includes: **I am Kevin, Vanya, Dear England, CLAN.**

Shankho Chaudhuri (Designer)

For the Royal Court: **Living Newspaper.**

As associate set & graphic designer, for the Royal Court: **Is God Is.**

Other theatre includes: **Alice in Wonderland (& Poltergeist), Kabul Goes Pop: Music Television Afghanistan (Brixton House); Macbeth: Something Wicked (Donmar/ Schools tour); Here, Here, Here (Stratford East); Five Plays (Young Vic); Final Farewell (Tara Theatre); Inside (Orange Tree); Art Heist (Poltergeist/New Diorama/ Underbelly); Wood, White Noise (VAULT).**

As associate set designer: **The Witches, Othello (National).**

As design assistant: **Death of England: Delroy, Death of England (National).**

As co-designer, dance includes: **Traplord (Sadlers Wells/180 Studios/Factory International/Altruviolet).**

Film includes: **The Magic Finger (Unicorn/ Roald Dahl).**

XR includes: **Through The Cracks (English Touring Theatre); Ghost Walk (Poltergeist /New Diorama/Broadgate); All Kinds of Limbo (National Immersive Storytelling Studio).**

As creative director, music includes: **Arrivals (Shangri-La, Glastonbury).**

Awards include: **Olivier Award for Best New Dance Production 2023 (Traplord), Untapped Award (Art Heist).**

Shankho was Staff Associate Designer at New Diorama (2021-22) and Resident Design Assistant at the National (2019 - 20).

Marc Elliott (Vic)

Theatre includes: **A Tupperware of Ashes, The Father and the Assassin, NT50, The History Boys (& West End) (National); The Deep Blue Sea (Ustinov Studio); O Let Us Howl! (Shipwright's); Woman in Mind (Chichester Festival); She Loves Me (Sheffield Crucible); [Title of Show] (Lambert Jackson); City of Angels, The Girl on the train, Urinetown, Tape (West End); Macbeth (Sam Wanamaker); Sweet Charity (Nottingham Playhouse); The Big I Am, Othello, Paint Your Wagon (Liverpool Everyman); Into the Woods (Manchester**

Royal Exchange); City of Angels (Donmar); See What I Wanna See (Jermyn Street); Wild Turkey, The Maids, Miss Julie (Naach Theatre Company); Les Liaisons Dangereuses (Vienna's English Theatre); Romeo and Juliet (Festival Players); Two Souls on a Dirty Night (503); Lord of the Flies, Macbeth, The Winter's Tale, Julius Caesar (RSC).

Television includes: **Juice, Call the Midwife, Holby City, NT50, Midsomer Murders, Eastenders, The Invisibles, M.I. High, Lewis, The Bill, Mile High.**

Radio includes: **Maps for Lost Lovers, Bombay Talkie, The Tenth Man, Jadoo!, The Mob.**

Zac Gvi
(Composer & Co-Sound Designer)

Theatre includes: **Twelfth Night (RSC); The Cherry Orchard (Donmar); From Here On (Gecko/Good Chance); Richard III, A Midsummer Night's Dream, Titus Andronicus, The Merchant Of Venice, Twelfth Night (Globe); The Odyssey: The Underworld (National); The Winston Machine (Tour), Dinomania (59E59), Trap Street (Schaubühne), Still III, Dog Show (New Diorama); Make Good (Pentabus/tour); Trueman and the Arsonists (Roundhouse); Romeo & Juliet, Moulin Rouge (Secret Cinema).**

Awards include: **Off West End Award for Best Ensemble (Dog Show), Peter Brook Festival Award (Dog Show).**

Alison Halstead (Bridget)

For the Royal Court: **Hole.**

Other theatre includes: **Princess Essex (Globe); The Cherry Orchard, Hamlet (Theatre Royal Windsor); Primary Shakespeare: Hamlet (National); The Provoked Wife, Venice Preserved (RSC); Future Bodies (HOME/Rash Dash/Unlimited); Julius Caesar (Sheffield Theatres); The House of Bernarda Alba (Graeae/Royal Exchange); Blood Wedding (Graeae/Dundee Rep); Exhibit B (Barbican); Prometheus Awakes (Graeae/La Fura dels Baus); Macbeth, As You Like It, King John (Chicago Shakespeare); Antigone, No Place Like Home (Steppenwolf); Aida (ENO); Wondrous Strange (& RSC), Falling Up (& National) (Mimbre Acrobatic).**

Television includes: **Citadel.**

Film includes: **Dune 2, Dimensions, Love Your Mama.**

Grace Hans
(Deputy Stage Manager)

For the Royal Court: **Cowbois (& RSC).**

Other theatre includes: **The Cat and the Canary (Chichester Festival); Wedding Band: A Love/Hate Story in Black and White, Raymond Briggs' Father Christmas (Lyric); Akedah (Hampstead); A Gig for Ghosts (Soho); We Will Be Happy Here (Albany); I Know I Know I Know (Southwark Playhouse); The Winston Machine (New Diorama); I Don't Know Why I'm Crying (Camden People's Theatre & Theatre Deli).**

Kirsty MacDiarmid
(Stage Manager)

Theatre includes: **Huddle (Filskrit/Unicorn); The Wind in the Willows (Theatre on Kew/ Australian Shakespeare Company); The Princess and the Pea (Upswing/ Unicorn/NYC); The Play That Goes Wrong (West End); Peaky Blinders the Redemption of Thomas Shelby (Rambert/ Tour); Dead Air (Stockroom); Bat Out of Hell (UK Tour); Little Scratch (Hampstead); The Hound of The Baskervilles (Yvonne Arnaud); Comedy of Errors (RSC); Ghost Quartet (Boulevard); Henry V and Tempest (Shakespeare's Rose York); The Cat in the Hat (Leicester Curve/Tour); The Oscar Wilde Season (Vaudeville/Classic Spring); Sweet Bird of Youth/The Norman Conquests (Chichester Festival Theatre); Paradise of the Assassins (Tara); Some Girls (Buckland Park 90); Running Wild (Regents Park Open Air); Othello and The Merchant of Venice (Playing Shakespeare/ Globe); Communicating Doors and What's it all about? (Menier Chocolate Factory); A Man of No Importance (Salisbury Playhouse); Our Friends the Enemy (Tremers/The Space); Wild Oats and Does my Society look big in this (Bristol Old Vic).**

Opera includes: **Grimes on the Beach (Aldeburgh Music); Faramondo (RCM)**

Lewis Mackinnon (Mike)

For the Royal Court: **Kid a Kidder, Anna Karenina (Pegasus).**

Other theatre includes: **Black Sheep (curious directive), Deciphering (New Diorama), Your Last Breath (Southwark) (curious directive); Miles (Riverside Studios), The Night Watch (York Theatre Royal/UK Tour) (Original Theatre Co); Sonnet Sunday (Globe); Three Sisters (Belfast Lyric Theatre); I'm Not That Kind of Guy (& Paines Plough), Keep Smiling (Play Theatre); Three Sisters, Goodnight Mr Bear (Squint/Etch/Pleasance); Gifted (503/Old Red Lion); Black Sheep (Soho).**

Television includes: **Young Wallander, Doctors, Victoria.**

Film includes: **The Longest Distance, The Sin-Eater, The Thing That Ate the Birds, Attrition, Dragonheart: Battle for the Heartfire, The Wyrd, The Wind from Nowhere, Chosen.**

Tim McMullan (Harry)

Theatre includes: **Mnemonic, Drive Your Plough Over the Bones of the Dead, The Master and Margarita, The Noise of Time, Light, Three Lives of Lucie Cabrol (Complicite); The Tempest, As You Like It (Globe); Hapgood (Hampstead); King Charles II, The Misanthrope, The Deep Blue Sea (West End); Father and Sons, The Front Page (Donmar); Neville's Island (Chichester Festival Theatre); A Flea in her Ear (Old Vic); Arabian Nights, The New Tenant (Young Vic); Anthony and Cleopatra, Twelfth Night, The Cherry Orchard, Burnt By The Sun, Present Laughter, Coram Boy, The Alchemist, Once in a Lifetime, His Dark Materials, The Three Sisters, The Caucasian Chalk Circle, Murmuring Judges, The Miser, The Resistible Rise of Arturo UI, Racing Demon, Wind in the Willows, Richard III (National); Theatre of Blood (Improbable); A Midsummer Night's Dream (RSC); Lady Betty (Cheek by Jowl).**

Television includes: **Moonflower Murders, Magpie Murders, The Crown, Brexit, Melrose, King Charles III, Fearless, The Witness for the Prosecution, Doctor Thorne, Granchester, The Go-Between, Foyle's War, Elementary, Endeavour, The Hollow Crown – Henry IV, Parade's End,**

Silk, Sense and Sensibility, Trial and Retribution, Pinochet in Suburbia, The Wimbledon Poisoner, Stalagluft.

Film includes: **Fackham Hall, Enola Holmes 2, The Woman in Black, The Queen, Two Men went to War, Eisenstein, Onegin, Shakespeare in Love, Plunkett and Maclean, Dangerous Beauty, The Fifth Element, Caught in the Act, Being Human, Shadowlands, Princess Caraboo, Victoria and Abdul.**

Isobel Pellow
(Costume Supervisor)

As costume supervisor, theatre includes: **Princess Essex (Globe); Kathy and Stella Solve A Murder (West End); Bronco Billy (Charing Cross); Jack and the Beanstalk (Stratford East); The Ballad of Hattie and James, Mlima's Tale, Retrograde, Girl on an Altar (Kiln); The Walworth Farce (Southwark Playhouse); A Christmas Carole (Southend Palace); Alice in Wonderland (Brixton House); The Memory of Water, Blackout Songs (Hampstead); Urinetown (Royal Academy of Music); The Sweet Science of Bruising (Wilton's Music Hall); Five Plays (Young Vic); Britten in Brooklyn (Wilton's Music Hall); Four Play, Clickbait (Theatre 503).**

Dance includes: **House of Flamenka (West End).** Opera includes Green Eggs and Ham (Opera North); The Crowning of Poppea (Jackson's Lane).

As costume designer, theatre includes: **Twelfth Night (Theatre on Kew); Death Drop (West End and UK Tour); Yes So I Said Yes, Not Quite Jerusalem, The Wind of Heaven (Finborough); Lysistrata (The Cockpit); Heather and Harry (Camden People's Theatre); King Lear (Pleasure Dome Theatre Company); 'Tis Pity She's A Whore (Tristan Bates); Three Brothers (Theatre N16); The Xmas Carol (Old Red Lion).**

Dance includes: **The Lay of the Land (The Place).** Opera includes Tales of Offenbach (Wilton's Music Hall).

Danusia Samal (Ghost Bridget)

For the Royal Court: **B, Maryland, How to Hold Your Breath.**

Other theatre includes: **Bangers (& Cardboard Citizens), Busking It (& Shoreditch Town Hall/HighTide), Billy the Girl (& Clean Break) (Soho); Peggy For You (Hampstead); Noah & the Peacock (Nottingham Playhouse); Rutherford & Son (Sheffield Crucible); Trap Street (Kandinsky); What If Women Ruled The World? (MIF); The Two Noble Kinsmen, The Rover (RSC); The Odyssey: Missing Presumed Dead (ETT/Liverpool Everyman); The House That Will Not Stand, Circles (& Birmingham Rep) (Kiln); The Birthday Party (Royal Exchange); 1001 Nights, Liar Liar (Unicorn); After The Rainfall (Curious Directive).**

Television includes: **Gangs of London, The Hack, The Serial Killer's Wife, Black Cake, The Great, Tyrant, Boom!.**

Film includes: **The Trip, Ghost in the Shell, My Friend the Polish Girl, Do You Want to Try Again?.**

Radio includes: **The Missed Lives of Max & Judy, Yusuf & The Whale, Black Water, Stalingrad, The Rage, The Skriker, The Odyssey: Missing Presumed Dead, Dr Who: Aquitane.**

Helen Schlesinger (Davina)

For the Royal Court: **The Stone, Wild East, The Weather, Bear Hug.**

Other theatre includes: **Richard III, Henry V, Henry IV Parts 1 & 2, Hamlet, As You Like It (Globe); Straight Line Crazy (Bridge); Albion (Almeida); Boys Will Be Boys, Whipping It Up (& West End) (Bush); Frozen (Park); Coriolanus (Donmar); Bracken Moor (Tricycle); Fireface (Young Vic); Skane, Comfort Me With Apples, (Hampstead); The Gods Weep, The Crucible (& West End), The Merchant of Venice, Twelfth Night (RSC); Messiah (Old Vic); The Oresteia, War and Peace, An Inspector Calls (& West End), Inadmissable Evidence (National); Mill on the Floss (Shared Experience); A Moon for the Misbegotten, Uncle Vanya, The Illusion, The Road to Mecca (Royal Exchange).**

Television includes: **We Might Regret This, Trying, Midsomer Murders, Lewis, Merlin, Eastenders, The Hour, Nativity, Criminal Justice, Sensitive Skin, Trial and Retribution, Bad Girls, The Way We Live Now, The Greatest Store on Earth.**

Film includes: **Dirty War, Twenty Four Hour Party People, Persuasion.**

Osnat Schmool
(Vocal Music Director)

As music director, theatre includes: **The Grapes of Wrath, The Crucible (& Gielgud), The Welkin (National); Grind (Tête à Tête Opera); A Christmas Carol (Pegasus).** As composer, **Macbeth (Shakespeare's Globe); Earth Makes No Sound, Momo, OSPEDALE, Under One Roof, Rufus, Drive Ride Walk (Filament); Goldilocks (Little Angel); Re:Love (Bridewell).**

As conductor: **Meltdown festival choirs for M.I.A and Guy Garvey (Southbank); Voices Now Choral Festival; Jamie Cullum's Late Night Prom.**

Awards include: **UK Folk Award - Best Traditional Track.**

Ryan Joseph Stafford
(Lighting Designer)

Theatre includes: **Olion (Frân Wen); Splinter (Sherman, Cardiff); Snakes & Ladders (Southwark Playhouse); Rope (Theatr Clwyd); Swim, Aunty, Swim (Belgrade); Hir (Park); Bacon (Riverside Studios, International Tour); Breeding (King's Head); Grimeboy (Birmingham Rep); Isla (Theatr Clwyd); Cyrano de Bergerac, Easy Virtue (The Watermill); Crave, Cardiff Boy (The Other Room, Cardiff); The Island (Fio, UK Tour); The Secret Lives of Baba Segi's Wives (Arcola).**

Dance includes: **Kontakthof: Echoes of '78 (Tanztheater Wuppertal Pina Bausch); Can This Place be a Temple? (The Place, UK Tour); TRAPLORD (Southbank); Natalia Osipova: Force of Nature (New York City Center, International Tour); Vortex (Russell Maliphant Dance Company, UK Tour); To Start With, Shades of Blue, Together, not the same (Sadler's); Codi (National Dance Company Wales, National Tour); Greater than Lion (Messums Gallery); Generation Goldfish (Bayerisches Staatsballett); Left from Write (Norwegian National Ballet, European Tour).**

Awards include: **Off West End Award for Best Lighting Design (Bacon), Michael Northern Award for Excellence in Lighting Design (Association of Lighting Designers).**

THE ROYAL COURT THEATRE

The Royal Court Theatre is the writers' theatre. It is a leading force in world theatre for cultivating and supporting writers - undiscovered, emerging and established.

Since 1956, we have commissioned and produced hundreds of writers, from John Osborne to Mohamed-Zain Dada. Royal Court plays from every decade are now performed on stages and taught in classrooms and universities across the globe.

Through the writers, the Royal Court is at the forefront of creating restless, alert, provocative theatre about now. We open our doors to the unheard voices and free thinkers that, through their writing, change our way of seeing.

We strive to create an environment in which differing voices and opinions can co-exist. In current times, it is becoming increasingly difficult for writers to write what they want or need to write without fear, and we will do everything we can to rise above a narrowing of viewpoints.

Through all our work, we strive to inspire audiences and influence future writers with radical thinking and provocative discussion.

🐦 royalcourt ▉ royalcourttheatre

ARTS COUNCIL
ENGLAND

Supported using public funding by

Kandinsky

'No-one else makes theatre quite like this' Time Out

Kandinsky makes and tours live theatre nationally and internationally. We believe in theatre as a force for collaboration and transformation, and our work aims to delight, challenge and surprise our audiences, young and old.

Our previous credits include: Dog Show, New Diorama Theatre (winner: OffWestEnd Award, Peter Brook Festival Award); Trap Street, New Diorama Theatre (transferred to Festival of International New Drama at the Schaubühne, Berlin); There Is a Light That Never Goes Out, Royal Exchange Theatre, Manchester; SHTF, Schauspielhaus Wien; and The Winston Machine, New Diorama & UK tour to venues including Theatre by the Lake, Marlowe Theatre, Bristol Old Vic.

Kandinsky is run by James Yeatman and Lauren Mooney.

www.kandinsky-online.com

ROYAL COURT SUPPORTERS

Our incredible community of supporters makes it possible for us to achieve our mission of nurturing and platforming writers at every stage of their careers. Our supporters are part of our essential fabric – they help to give us the freedom to take bigger and bolder risks in our work, develop and empower new voices, and create world-class theatre that challenges and disrupts the theatre ecology.

To all our supporters, thank you. You help us to write the future.

PUBLIC FUNDING

Supported using public funding by
ARTS COUNCIL ENGLAND

CHARITABLE PARTNERS

The Common Humanity Arts Trust

BackstageTrust

COCKAYNE

T. S. Eliot
T. S. ELIOT FOUNDATION

JERWOOD FOUNDATION

CORPORATE SPONSORS & SUPPORTERS
Aqua Financial Ltd
Cadogan
Concord Theatricals
Edwardian Hotels, London
NJA Ltd. – Core Values & Creative Management
Nick Hern Books
Prime Time
Sustainable Wine Solutions
Walpole
Phone Locker

SISTER

CORPORATE MEMBERS
Bloomberg Philanthopies
Sloane Stanley

TRUSTS & FOUNDATIONS

Maria Björnson Memorial Fund
Martin Bowley Charitable Trust
Bruce Wake Charitable Trust
Chalk Cliff Trust
The Noël Coward Foundation
Cowley Charitable Foundation
The Davidson Play GC Bursary
The Fenton Arts Trust
Garrick Charitable Trust
The Golsoncott Foundation
The Lynne Gagliano Writers' Award
The Harold Hyam Wingate Foundation
John Lyon's Charity
The Marlow Trust
Clare McIntyre's Bursary
Old Possum's Practical Trust
Richard Radcliffe Charitable Trust
Rose Foundation
The Royal Borough of Kensington & Chelsea Arts Grant
Royal Victoria Hall Foundation
Theatres Trust
The Thistle Trust
The Thompson Family Charitable Trust
Unity Theatre Trust

INDIVIDUAL SUPPORTERS

Artistic Director's Circle

Eric Abraham
Katie Bradford
Jeremy & Becky Broome
Clyde Cooper
Debbie De Girolamo &
Ben Babcock
Dominique & Neal Gandhi
Lydia & Manfred Gorvy
David & Jean Grier
Charles Holloway OBE
Linda Keenan
Andrew Rodger and Ariana
Neumann
Jack Thorne & Rachel Mason
Sandra Treagus for
ATA Assoc. LTD
Sally Whitehill & Mark Gordon
Anonymous

Writers' Circle

Chris & Alison Cabot
Cas Donald
Robyn Durie
Ellie & Roger Guy
Melanie J. Johnson
Nicola Kerr
Héloïse and Duncan
Matthews KC
Emma O'Donoghue
Clare Parsons & Tony Langham
Maureen & Tony Wheeler
Anonymous

Directors' Circle

Piers Butler
Fiona Clements
Professor John Collinge
Julian & Ana Garel-Jones
Carol Hall
Dr Timothy Hyde

Platinum Circle

Moira Andreae
Tyler Bollier
Katie Bullivant
Anthony Burton CBE
Matthew Dean
Emily Fletcher
Beverley Gee
Damien Hyland
Susanne Kapoor
David P Kaskel &
Christopher A Teano
Peter & Maria Kellner
Robert Ledger &
Sally Moulsdale
Frances Lynn
Mrs Janet Martin
Andrew McIver
Brian & Meredith Niles
Corinne Rooney
Anita Scott
Bhags Sharma
Dr Wendy Sigle
Rita Skinner
Brian Smith
Mrs Caroline Thomas
Ian, Victoria & Lucinda Watson
Sir Robert & Lady Wilson
Beverley Buckingham
The Edwin Fox Foundation
Lucy and Spencer De Grey
Madeleine Hodgkin
Barbara Minto
Timothy Prager
Sir Paul & Lady Ruddock
James and Victoria Tanner
Yannis Vasatis
Anonymous

With thanks to our Silver and Gold Supporters, and our Friends and Good Friends, whose support we greatly appreciate.

Let's be friends. With benefits.

Our Friends and Good Friends are part of the fabric of the Royal Court. They help us to create world-class theatre, and in return they receive early access to our shows and a range of exclusive benefits.

Join today and become a part of our community.

Become a Friend (from £40 a year)

Benefits include:
- Priority Booking
- Advanced access to £15 Monday tickets
- 10% Bar & Kitchen discount (including Court in the Square)

Become a Good Friend (from £95 a year)

In addition to the Friend benefits, our Good Friends also receive:

- Five complimentary playtexts for Royal Court productions
- An invitation for two to step behind the scenes of the Royal Court Theatre at a special event

Our Good Friends' membership also includes a voluntary donation. This extra support goes directly towards supporting our work and future, both on and off stage.

To become a Friend or a Good Friend, or to find out more about the different ways in which you can get involved, visit our website: royalcourttheatre. com/support-us

The English Stage Company at the Royal Court Theatre is a registered charity (No. 231242)

MORE LIFE

Lauren Mooney and James Yeatman
for Kandinsky Theatre Company

Characters

CHORUS 1–6
ROBOT
BRIDGET
DAVINA
EVE
ROGER
ELOISE
HARRY
CHRISTOPHER
HENRY
PAST BRIDGET
NINA
MIKE
TYRONE
BETTY
VICTOR

Note on the Text

/ means the next speaker begins talking from that point.

[text inside square brackets means something thought but unspoken.]

… at the end of speech means it trails off.

+ indicates that we are cutting between scenes which in reality are not happening in the same time or place.

Note on Doubling

More Life is a play for an ensemble of six performers. Doubling should be as follows:

Chorus 1
Robot
Bridget

Chorus 2
Davina
Eve
Roger
Eloise

Chorus 3
Harry
Christopher
Henry

Chorus 4
Past Bridget
Nina

Chorus 5
Mike
Tyrone
Betty

Chorus 6
Victor

This text went to press before the end of rehearsals and so may differ slightly from the play as performed.

ACT ONE

1. PROLOGUE

Darkness, or some kind of non-electric light. The CHORUS
enters. They make sound, foley and music alongside the text.

1   Tuesday the eighteenth of January, 1803. A mild,
           wet winter. The rain starts as they drag George
           Foster's body from the gallows.

2   You can't always be sure with these things, but
           he's definitely dead.

           We hear a choking noise.

3   Hangings at Newgate are still public. Foster's
           friends in the crowd stood close to the scaffold and
           when the trapdoor opened, they gathered round his
           kicking legs, and pulled.

           A broken neck. A kind of mercy. They're not
           invited to the after-party.

4   This is England in 1803, where the bodies of
           convicted murderers belong to the state. Foster's
           sentence wasn't only to be hanged:

           it was to be hanged and dissected.

           We're twenty years from Burke and Hare, but
           medical science is advancing at an astonishing
           rate, and doctors need corpses.

           We hear a neck-break noise.

5   There's also a moral function.

           It's widely believed that dissected bodies are too
           mutilated for the condemned to rise again on
           Judgement Day.

To be hanged for murder in England in 1803 is to lose not just your human life, but your immortal one, too.

3   'One, two, three – '

They make noises of carrying.

6   George Foster's body is taken to a house several streets from Newgate, and laid out there, on the scrubbed wooden table.

3   'Okay, put him down'

4   It is a room not very like this one, but still, there is a stage, of a kind.

A stage and an audience.

CHORUS 4 *becomes Aldini.*

2   A respectful hush falls. This is the man they've been waiting for.

6   Not Foster. Poor, dead George Foster's just a prop.

5   They've come to see the great physicist himself: Signor Aldini.

3   Aldini has a famous uncle, Luigi Galvani, from whom we derive the word 'galvanise': 'to shock something into action'. All of this is his idea. But Galvani only ever got to try it on frogs.

5   The men in that room hold their breath.

Everyone holds their breath.

1   It's hot, with all of them packed in together.

3   Hot, and dark,

2   as Aldini attaches the conducting rods to a large electrical battery.

4/Aldini plugs a mic in. We hear a buzz and hum – for the first time made by piped-in sound rather than the company.

6   The hum of it. The fizz. The smell in that room.

5   Hot copper, rubber piping, and death.

1   And finally it's time:

         They watch Aldini lay the conducting rod against
         George Foster's face.

         We hear electronic music, building.

6   There won't be electric light in England for
         another seventy years.

5   When the current passes through the dead man's
         face, it twitches.

2   For a moment, his eye opens; the corpse on the
         table seems to wink.

3   Some of the men in the audience are curious;
         some are sceptics;

1   some believe that they are literally about to watch
         a hanged man be restored to life.

3   A hand reaching beyond the vale, into The
         Unknown.

2   The vale reaches back. Within an hour, one of the
         men in this audience will be dead, a heart attack.

5   The newspapers will say he died of fright.

6   Aldini moves his conducting rod across George
         Foster's lifeless body.

1   As the current passes through his right hand,

         They gasp.

3   it rises from the table.

         Noise, electronic music, singing.

2   A clenched fist beating the air. His legs twitch. His
         thighs convulse.

         CHORUS 4 *speaks into the mic.*

4   The invention of the telegraph is coming. The first
           radio transmission. The first computer. A century
           from now, electricity will be fully known,
           harnessed and tamed. This is what the future looks
           like: a dead man twitching on a table. The end of
           all life's mysteries. The end of death itself. It starts
           here in this room.

           Everything cuts out. Silence.

1   Two hundred and seventy years later, the door of
           the Edius Labs facility slides open, and someone
           wheels the machine-body inside. It is an empty
           vessel. Lifeless.

6   And then it isn't.

2. THE LAB

CHORUS 1 *becomes the* ROBOT *and stands in the space with*
VICTOR. *Everyone else is gathered round the edge, each at a*
microphone.

The project is to upload different scanned brains to the ROBOT,
to see if they function. Each new speaker is voiced by the
indicated chorus member into a mic, while 1/ROBOT *lip-syncs.*

A sound indicates the uploading of consciousness to the robot,
and there is another one for it being switched off. The on/off
sounds start to blur together as the scene goes on.

Eve

ON sound.

VICTOR   Eve?

            Are you awake?

EVE   Yes

VICTOR	Can you hear me?
EVE	Yes
VICTOR	How does it feel?
EVE	Feel?
	It feels
	I
VICTOR	Okay, you don't have to answer that yet.
	What do you remember?
EVE	I
	I don't
VICTOR	Eve?
EVE	Eve?
VICTOR	That's you
EVE	Eve
VICTOR	Yes
	That's you
	Do you / want to
EVE	I remember water
VICTOR	Yes?
EVE	The feeling of water
	Weightless
	Floating
	That's how it feels
VICTOR	Now?
EVE	Yes
VICTOR	Okay
EVE	But

	No
	It's
VICTOR	Can you tell me what else you remember?
EVE	It's not like that
VICTOR	Eve –
EVE	It's like nothing
	It's nothing
	I don't feel anything
VICTOR	But you're not in any pain?
EVE	Pain?
	No.
VICTOR	Good. That's good.
EVE	I remember
VICTOR	What?
EVE	I remember
	Fire
VICTOR	Mm. That can't be good.
EVE	I remember fire
VICTOR	Mike?
EVE	I remember pain
VICTOR	Mike, are you / getting this
EVE	I remember, I'm
	/ Please
VICTOR	Mike!
	OFF sound.
	Thanks
	Subject B351-4 remembers its death

So

We should make a note of that, yeah?

Right. Next

Christopher

ON sound.

VICTOR   Christopher

Are you awake?

Can you hear me?

(*To* MIKE.) Are we getting consciousness readings? Because if not

CHRISTOPHER   No

VICTOR   Christopher?

You can hear us, can't you?

How does it feel?

CHRISTOPHER   No

VICTOR   Okay

CHRISTOPHER   No

VICTOR   Okay, Christopher, don't panic

CHRISTOPHER   No

no

no

no

VICTOR   It's important to try to remain calm

CHRISTOPHER   No no no no no / no no no no

VICTOR   / Christopher?

CHRISTOPHER   no no no no

VICTOR   Mike, I don't think this one's going to –

CHRISTOPHER   / nonononononono

VICTOR   Er

Yeah, let's switch it off

OFF sound.

Lewis

ON sound.

VICTOR   Lewis?

Lewis, can you hear me?

Lewis?

Mike

OFF sound.

Yep

Tyrone

TYRONE *wakes up and begins talking without interruption, a constant stream-of-consciousness. He does not see or respond to* VICTOR.

TYRONE   the day was sunny so I went to the shops and
I thought I'd get a cauliflower and a beetroot
because I thought I might roast them to make
couscous or some other Mediterranean vegetable
dish possibly it could have feta or raisins and a
squeeze of lemon

VICTOR   / Tyrone?

Tyrone? Can you? Ty–

TYRONE   but in the shop they had none of those things
the shopkeeper was old and hunched but had a
baby kitten in his lap and he was shelling peas

into a bowl and instead I thought I'd have some aubergines but they were rotten and the corn on the cob was bad and the salad leaves were quite swampy so I thought instead I'd have a baked potato but even they'd seen better days

VICTOR   (*To* MIKE.) Stop

OFF/ON noise.

Nina

NINA *is performing a physical action. Poised and delicate. She has the manners of an older lady.*

VICTOR   That's really good Nina

NINA   Yeah?

VICTOR   You're doing well

NINA   Thanks. Thank you

VICTOR   I'd like to do some more tests now, is that okay?

NINA   It's weird, not breathing

VICTOR   Yeah. You just have to relax

It's important you don't fight it. The body

NINA   No

VICTOR   It's a new start for you

NINA   Yeah

I wanted this

VICTOR   Yeah?

NINA   I gave permission. I remember

Before I died, they made me / sign all these forms

VICTOR   (*Interrupting.*) Great! Great

It's really good you remember that, Nina

Giving permission

	But I'd like you to look back earlier, is that okay?
NINA	Earlier?
VICTOR	Yeah. Much earlier
NINA	You mean before I / died?
VICTOR	*Yes* Nina. Erm
	Do you remember your childhood?
NINA	Childhood?
VICTOR	What do you remember about it?
	Nina?
NINA	I…
	I…
VICTOR	Anything at all?
NINA	I
	Don't
VICTOR	Ah.

VICTOR *makes a gesture to* MIKE. *She's no good.*

OFF/ON.

Samuel

SAMUEL *falls on the floor. There are no signs of life.*

OFF/ON.

Henry

HENRY *is lying on the floor.*

HENRY	I can.
VICTOR	You can't.
HENRY	I can.

VICTOR	Prove it.
HENRY	I don't want to
	I don't want to stand up yet.
VICTOR	Yeah because you can't. You can't work the body.
HENRY	Yes, I can.
VICTOR	Go on then.
	I don't believe you.
HENRY	Listen, Doctor Whoever-You-Are –
VICTOR	I'm not a doctor.
HENRY	Right, well maybe that's the problem.
	I'd like to speak to a doctor, please
	A real one.
	OFF/ON.

Betty

BETTY is up and about, doing some kind of flapping thing with her arms.

BETTY	No arms
VICTOR	No, that's not right
BETTY	No arms
VICTOR	(*To* MIKE.) I've told her
	Betty?
BETTY	No arms
VICTOR	No, Betty. You do / have arms
BETTY	No arms
VICTOR	Okay
BETTY	No arms

VICTOR   Mike?

BETTY   No arms

            No arms

            OFF/ON.

Roger

ROGER *sings an eighties song in the club style, something like 'Club Tropicana' by Wham!. He is unresponsive to* VICTOR.

OFF/ON.

Bridget

This feels different.

4/PAST BRIDGET *speaks.* 1/BRIDGET *lip-syncs.*

PAST BRIDGET   I like spicy foods. I like to cook. I'm a teacher. I'm married. We live in the city. I sleep badly at night. I'm a cat person. I like jogging. I find long walks boring. I like to move quickly. I'm not very patient

                     I remember my childhood.

VICTOR   / Okay

PAST BRIDGET   I remember the sound of the ocean. I remember the desks in our classroom, the year my first teeth / fell out

VICTOR   Bridget, you can stop. You can stop now

PAST BRIDGET   I'm sorry.

                     Was that too much?

VICTOR   No. It was very good. You're doing well

PAST BRIDGET   Thanks.

VICTOR   And how do you feel?

PAST BRIDGET   Calm.

VICTOR   I mean physically.

PAST BRIDGET   Physically?

VICTOR   How do you feel, physically?

PAST BRIDGET   Oh. Fine

VICTOR   No pain?

PAST BRIDGET   No. Why?

VICTOR   I'd like you to try and walk for me.

PAST BRIDGET   Did something happen to me?

VICTOR   Did

PAST BRIDGET   To my body? It doesn't feel

VICTOR   Yes, Bridget. It did.

Is that okay?

Beat.

You have a new body.

PAST BRIDGET   Yes.

VICTOR   Can you lift your arm?

She does. Music.

Do you still feel calm?

PAST BRIDGET   I don't know. It's strange. Like a dream.

VICTOR   But you're not panicking

PAST BRIDGET   No.

VICTOR   That's good, Bridget. You're doing great

PAST BRIDGET   Thanks

VICTOR   You moved your arm so well that, now, I'm going to ask you to walk for me.

Do you think you can do that?

PAST BRIDGET   Sure

VICTOR   You might find you need to think about it harder than you used to

But try.

Think about putting one leg in front of the other.

She walks. Music again. It feels momentous.

She stops.

1/ROBOT/BRIDGET *should now speak with their own voice.*

BRIDGET   Can I see my husband now?

VICTOR   Your? Oh

BRIDGET   He'll be worried. He gets anxious if he doesn't hear from me.

VICTOR   Does he?

BRIDGET   What's wrong?

VICTOR   What do you mean?

BRIDGET   You seem like you're –

Like someone hiding bad news.

VICTOR   Oh

BRIDGET   Because I mean – if there was bad news, I'd / rather you just

VICTOR   No, okay, let's –

Let's stop a second.

There's – [*a right order to do these things in.*]

Let's just take a deep breath, shall we?

CHORUS 4 *makes the sound of breathing.*

I mean, figuratively.

It doesn't stop.

Bridget, I understand that you have questions. And
we're going to answer them, I assure you. But
you need to be patient just a little longer. Now,
I've seen your file – I know that you were clever,
logical – so you can / understand

BRIDGET   Were?

VICTOR   What?

BRIDGET   Did you say 'were'?

VICTOR   I said

'are.'

I said that you're – clever, logical, are those
things. Okay?

So I know you can appreciate that we're doing
everything in a very specific order, for a very
specific reason. And you can trust that when the /
time comes

BRIDGET   Am I dead?

Beat. The breath.

VICTOR   Bridget –

BRIDGET   Am I?

VICTOR   How would I be talking to you / now, if

BRIDGET   But you said 'were'

VICTOR   I'm trying to tell you there's a process

BRIDGET   Oh god. I am, aren't I? I'm dead

VICTOR   There's no need to get upset

BRIDGET   This is hell. / I'm in

VICTOR   Of course it – listen to me, of course it's not hell.
Christ!

BRIDGET   But you won't answer the question, you / won't
actually

VICTOR	Bridget
	We hear a heartbeat.
BRIDGET	You're scaring me, you're really
VICTOR	No, no I'm not, because there's nothing to be frightened of, okay?
BRIDGET	It's not mine. None of it feels like my
VICTOR	We'll sit down. We'll talk. There's a process
	CHORUS 4 *breathing harder, almost hyperventilating.*
BRIDGET	My chest hurts
VICTOR	I promise you, it doesn't
BRIDGET	Because I'm dead, that's what you're saying
VICTOR	Let's not get hysterical
BRIDGET	I can't breathe
VICTOR	You don't need to
BRIDGET	No, I mean I can't, I mean, my chest, it – hurts –
	Breathing.
VICTOR	No it doesn't
BRIDGET	Yes it does!
VICTOR	Ah
	Okay. I've seen this before. This is –
	Bridget, this is just your brain 'remembering' panic
BRIDGET	Answer the question
VICTOR	But you don't actually need to breathe any more, so the feeling –
BRIDGET	/ Please
VICTOR	this feeling, it's just your mind playing tricks. Okay?

BRIDGET   Victor, did I fucking die?

Beat.

VICTOR   Yes.

The breathing is loud. Like a panic attack.

Bridget?

BRIDGET   I think I'm going to

Pass out

VICTOR   Right. You might think that, but you won't. You can't.

BRIDGET   When

VICTOR   When?

BRIDGET   When did I – how –

VICTOR   Oh. A long time ago. Back in like, 2026

BRIDGET   It is 2026

VICTOR   No. No, it's not, I'm afraid

BRIDGET   What the

VICTOR   So, let's do it then, let's get it all – Why not? Bridget, you were killed

Forty-eight years / ago, after a

BRIDGET   Fuck you

VICTOR   Actually I'm not totally sure / what the

BRIDGET   You bastard

VICTOR   Bridget.

BRIDGET   My family. My husband

No, I don't want this

VICTOR   We were doing really well

BRIDGET   I don't want it. I won't do it. Whatever this is

VICTOR   Mike?

BRIDGET   Some sick joke. I won't be part of – of –

VICTOR   Yeah, okay, switch her off

BRIDGET   What?

                    She is switched off.

                    VICTOR *is shaken.*

VICTOR   Yeah.

                    That was –

                    We were really close there.

                    Quiet. He looks at the body that was Bridget.

                    MIKE *is there.*

MIKE   You good, boss?

                    What you doing?

VICTOR   Reading her file

MIKE   Who?

VICTOR   B389-6. Bridget.

MIKE   Why are you doing that?

VICTOR   Ouch.

MIKE   What?

VICTOR   Hit by a car. A self-driving – one of the pilot tests.
                    Before they'd got the kinks worked out. That
                    explains the

                    MIKE *laughs.*

                    What?

MIKE   Nothing. Cars! Another world isn't it

VICTOR   Mike.

MIKE   Sorry. Erm

VICTOR   Permission to store deceased brain given by
                    next of kin, something something, terrible

handwriting – that must be the husband, the anxious one

MIKE   No point loading another now, is there?

VICTOR   We should look him up, find out if he's still alive – could be good for witness-confirmation

MIKE   Just cos I could do with getting away on time

VICTOR   Mike, are you listening? B389-6 Bridget – I'm asking you to find out if the next of kin is still alive, for external validation of intact / personality

MIKE   But

VICTOR   But what?

MIKE   But it's – it's over. She failed. We switched her off.

VICTOR   No

I want to –

Give me another go with her.

MIKE   What are you talking about?

VICTOR   New file, no short-term memory, start her off fresh, just –

MIKE   But

VICTOR   She was doing well. It was going to work.

MIKE   Vic

VICTOR   No, she was nearly it. The first.

She still can be.

MIKE   But it's not how we're / supposed to

VICTOR   Mike, I am your senior consultant. If I tell you to do something, what do you do?

MIKE   Okay, okay. Don't stress.

I'll wipe it, yeah?

We can try again in the morning. If that's what you really want.

VICTOR   It is.

MIKE   Sure. See you tomorrow then?

He sits back down. VICTOR *is left alone onstage.*

3. THE FUTURE

Music.

The CHORUS *speak from mics at the side of stage.*

3   And that's it. The end of another day.

4   'Bye Vic. Bye'

3   His colleagues

2   And Vic's out of the lab, through the endless long white hallways, the atrium, its vast golden light and –

5   'See you'

1   He lifts his face to the eye scanner –

2   Eye scanner?

1   Yes. Little red dots passing over his face

2   Lovely thought, obviously, but I don't think that's going to work.

     We should say a chip in the palm of the hand. Chips are better

1   But eye scanners are cool. Like a spy movie

2   You can do more with chips, though. Biometrics, data. You can know a lot about somebody.

1   But

2   So you could know about Victor, for instance, that his heart has been beating at an unusually elevated

rate for the last seventeen minutes. You could know he felt they were close to something, and the feeling hasn't gone away

4   He believes.

3   He places his biochipped palm on the / gate scanners

1   / eye scanners

5   Doo-doo

3   And then he's free.

        Out into the air. The night. The future

4   Wide shot of a cityscape. A man steps onto the rain-soaked pavement, glass doors sealing behind him

5   Whooosshhh

4   The building – private money, private aims – is scrupulously discreet

1   The man is tired

4   And the street – the street is –

5   There are roads in the sky.

4   No

5   Yeah. Sky-roads.

4   No, there wouldn't be roads. There wouldn't be cars. The future is walkable. Great domes of small-scale, organic, deeply rooted human communities / with

2   These are people we're talking about, not strawberries, / it's

3   It's a city. I think we should agree that it's a city

2/5   Yeah.

4   Yeah but is the sky still blue?

2	I'm sorry?
4	I read somewhere that the sky will be purple in the future. Something to do with climate / change, with
3	Well let's not get into that. It's night, it's dark, that's all we need to say about / that
4	But
1	Wide shot of a cityscape pouring with rain.
	Yes: in the future, it still rains. In the future there will still be cars, and oil-slick pavements, / and
5	Let's say it's a city skyline that looks like… I mean, Seoul? That's pretty futuristic
2	But English. Somewhere in England
4	Sure, but where? The Thames Barrier could be breached any time from 2030, right? So London's / probably underwater by
3	The future city! And it's all there, all of it –
	The sky-roads, the tubes funnelling people around at super-speed, the robots out on the street, the drones carrying parcels. The arc of the biodome refracting the street lights. The eco-skyscrapers with greenhouse balcony pods growing tomatoes. The neon lights of the city spread out like stars, the hiss of transport, mass of people moving at speed, all of it, the future, cooler than cool, and it's –
	Amazing.
1	Interior of a car
5	A flying car
1	Yes – interior of a flying car. Vic's sprawled on the back seat, watching the world pass by
2	All the time, the chip in his palm tracking his blood sugar, gut microbiome,

1   tracking his nutritional needs against the items in
        his fridge.

3   Some smart houses will do the cooking for you,
        but that's a bit gauche, really, isn't it?

5   Vic likes cooking. A lot of people do. And it's
        recommended as a mindfulness activity by most
        health-tracking devices, / so

4   So he gets home, and he cooks. Thinking, perhaps,
        as we all sometimes do:

3   Am I really going to have to go on feeding and
        moving and cleaning this body until I die?

        How unbelievably exhausting.

5   A lonely evening. Dinner for one, sprawled in
        front of the TV

2   The lights in the house dim.

1   Readying his nervous system for sleep.

4   Guiding him towards the bedroom.

        Beat.

3   And does he dream about her?

5   Who?

3   Bridget. Does he dream about Bridget? Her voice,
        her soul inside a magic box.

2   Her voice, her soul, her way of being in the world

1   her consciousness, waiting to live again, and he
        can do it. He can set her free.

5   In a manner of speaking.

2   yes – life, of a kind

1   Life inside a magic box. That looks like – what?

3   You mean the body? Well, it must be human –
        humanoid.

1   Wouldn't look like her though

3	No, not like she used to. I mean it's the generic one, isn't it? One size fits all
5	But human.
4	The human ideal
5	Six foot tall. Arms of a bodybuilder
3	Okay
5	A huge, masculine
2	Or a woman. The body might look like a woman's.
3	Or neither. Both. Because the consciousnesses
4	It'd probably look like Cate Blanchett. All these tech bros are obsessed with *Lord of the Rings*
5	Cate Blanchett, but with massive
2	The point is:
	Does he dream about it?
	The moment, the morning, the moment he gets to step back into his office at last at last at fucking last and –
	A loud BEEP, like the ON/OFF sounds from Scene 2, interrupts.

4. MULTIPLE CHOICE

We are back in the lab.

VICTOR   Bridget?

Bridget, are you awake?

Beat.

BRIDGET   Yes

VICTOR   Can you hear me?

BRIDGET   Yes

VICTOR   How do you feel?

BRIDGET   I feel

            Okay

VICTOR   Okay? That's good.

            I want you to relax.

            Tell me what you remember, from before. From…

            Is this what I said last time?

BRIDGET   / Last?

VICTOR   Mike, yes please.

BRIDGET   What?

            She's been shut down.

VICTOR   Sorry about that. I need to just –

            He does a few warm-up exercises.

            Okay. Can we start again?

BEEP.

A new Bridget.

She is walking.

VICTOR   That's great, Bridget. You're doing so well. You're
            really good at this.

BRIDGET   Thanks.

            Am I –

            Sorry, I don't know your name

VICTOR   It's Vic. Victor. Hi

BRIDGET   Victor. Did something happen to me?

VICTOR   Well

BRIDGET   Why do you look like that? You / look really

VICTOR   Let's not get

BRIDGET   cagey, I'm sorry but you do. It's unsettling

VICTOR   Listen

BEEP.

A new Bridget.

BRIDGET   But it is 2026

VICTOR   No. No, it's not, I'm afraid

BRIDGET   What the

BEEP.

A new Bridget.

VICTOR   I'm offering – information seems to be very
           important to you, you're always asking to be told
           what's going on, so / if you'd

BRIDGET   I'm listening, I'm

VICTOR   let me just –

BRIDGET   Fine. Go ahead.

VICTOR   Good.

           So, Bridget. Your brain was preserved at the
           moment of your death.

           It was stored in a very special kind of freezer.
           And eight months ago, following a technological
           breakthrough, it was taken out of that 'freezer',
           sliced into tiny, really quite remarkably small
           slivers, and each of those slivers was 'scanned'
           with a very complicated, incredibly expensive
           machine. All the proteins, the neurons, the neural
           pathways, it was all –

            Mapped. Known.

            Are you with me?

BRIDGET   I…

BEEP.

A new Bridget.

VICTOR   That version of your brain was created and saved to our 'hard drive', if you will.

            Imagine yourself as a file on a computer:

            That's you. That's what you are now.

BRIDGET   This is a joke.

VICTOR   I assure you, it isn't.

            And every time we to explain this to you, explain what a gift you've been given, / you react by

BRIDGET   Fuck you.

VICTOR   Right on time!

BEEP.

A new Bridget.

VICTOR *has a doll and a toy car.*

He hits them together. Tosses the doll away.

VICTOR   And that's how you died.

            A long pause.

BRIDGET   What the fuck?

BEEP.

A new Bridget.

MIKE *is there.*

BRIDGET   Who's that?

VICTOR   This is Mike. My boss.

MIKE   Hi.

VICTOR   He wants to switch you off.

BRIDGET   He wants to – what? Why?

VICTOR   He says you haven't progressed as expected. He
              thinks I've become fixated on the idea that you're
              going to be the first without enough real evidence
              to suggest that I'm right

BRIDGET   Is that true?

MIKE   Uh

              Yep.

BRIDGET   What do you mean, progressed as expected? I've
              just

              I've only just woken up.

MIKE   Well

BRIDGET   You said I was doing really well! You said my
              walking was great!

MIKE   Yes! But

              No.

              No, it's not working, Vic, I'm sorry.

VICTOR   Please

MIKE   Time to pull the plug I'm afraid

BRIDGET/VICTOR   No!

BRIDGET   I don't understand

VICTOR   Can I explain to her? Will you give me a moment to

BRIDGET   Please

MIKE   Fine. But do it quickly, Victor. Like I always say:
              Time Is Money

VICTOR   Bridget, I know it doesn't feel like it, but this is
              the seventh time we've woken you up

BRIDGET   The what

VICTOR   Yes, you see, we scanned your brain into a kind
of – something like a hard drive

BRIDGET   A

VICTOR   And we've been reloading your 'save file', if you
will, to the original, starting all over again, trying
to get you to – to accept

BRIDGET   what the / fuck

MIKE   Here we go –

No evidence of improvement, Vic, so I really do
think / it's time

VICTOR   Bridget, please don't let him do this to you. To us.
Okay?

BRIDGET   No.

No!

I don't want this. No, I reject this, I / reject this
whole thing

MIKE   / Ughhhh

VICTOR   / Bridget, no, please don't say that, because we'll
have to

BEEP.

A new Bridget.

BRIDGET   Who's that?

VICTOR   This is Mike. He works for me.

MIKE   Hi.

VICTOR   Show her what you've got there, Mike.

MIKE   Oh. This is – it's a control panel. For you.

BRIDGET   What?

VICTOR   Now, Bridget, I have been patient with you. I have
            been patient, and civil, and I have believed –
            I have believed in you. That costs me something.
            Do you understand?

BRIDGET   Not / really

VICTOR   We're offering you life, here, Bridget. The gift
            of – the *gift* –

            And you have been given chance after chance,
            but this is it, the end of the line. If you won't stay
            calm, and listen, Mike is going to switch you off,
            and we will never, ever turn you back on again.
            You will cease to exist.

BRIDGET   You fucking –

            MIKE *holds up the panel.*

            Don't. Just –

            Stop.

            Beat.

            This can't be real. It's a joke. Or some kind of

VICTOR   No.

            Listen to me, Bridget.

            You've done well. You've been able to accept
            your situation, up to a point. But we keep hitting
            this snag, and I'm just – I'm doing this for you!
            I'm trying to

BRIDGET   Can I ask questions?

VICTOR   What questions?

BRIDGET   I wasn't talking to you, I was talking to him.
            Mike?

MIKE   Er

VICTOR   No, talk to me. I'm the / one in charge

BRIDGET   But I don't / trust you

VICTOR   Okay, turn her off

BRIDGET   Mike, please

MIKE   Erm

BRIDGET   you just work here, right? You're just doing your job, so

VICTOR   We're doing this my way, by my rules, don't / you dare

MIKE   What do you want to know?

VICTOR   No, no, this isn't your place, Mike, give me the

           He goes to seize the device.

BRIDGET   I don't think so

           She takes it.

MIKE   Whoa whoa whoa

VICTOR   Bridget

BRIDGET   I just want to have a little chat with Mike!

MIKE   be careful. One slip and

BRIDGET   Don't worry about me, I have steady fucking hands, okay?

VICTOR   You're holding a gun to your own head, Bridget, / see if I care

BRIDGET   Yeah? And how much is it worth, a box like this? How much trouble would you get in if I crushed it? I can feel –

           This body, it's strong. I know I can do it.

           I could even just – slip –

MIKE   Stop!

BRIDGET   Yeah, thought so.

           Okay, Mike. So.

           There's got to be –

           Rules. You can't just do this to somebody

MIKE   No. No, you're right.

            Every test subject either gave permission, or
            permission was given by next of kin

BRIDGET   Test subject?

MIKE   People like you, whose / brains were

BRIDGET   Wait, are you saying my husband – he / let you

VICTOR   Mike, stop, this is deeply confidential information

BRIDGET   He wouldn't – he loved me. He wouldn't do this
            to me

MIKE   Well maybe he thought you wanted

VICTOR   Mike!

BRIDGET   You, stay out of this.

            Oh, god. Oh god I'm in hell

VICTOR   Now, you've said that before. An interestingly
            persistent belief, given your file doesn't say
            anything about you having been religious.

BRIDGET   What?

VICTOR   You had a humanist funeral, Bridget. I do hope
            that's what you would have wanted.

BRIDGET   I'm going to kill you

VICTOR   Oh but that's new. Interesting

BRIDGET   I'm going to kill your fucking boss, Mike

MIKE   Just be careful / with the device

BRIDGET   Fine, fine, fine!

MIKE   I think we should all just calm down. Vic, stop
            helping

BRIDGET   Fine.

MIKE   We were talking. We can talk. Bridget, if you have
            questions –

BRIDGET   Is he alive?

MIKE   Who?

BRIDGET   My husband. Is he – you said it's been – years –

MIKE   I don't know.

            But I can find out.

VICTOR   Mike

BRIDGET   Do it.

MIKE   Okay. But I need…

            Bridget, I need you to trust me. I won't let him
            have it. But that device you're holding…

            If you give it to me, I can call your file up. There
            are records, I'll be able to tell you if he's alive –
            but without it, I'm not / going to be

BRIDGET   I'll do it then. I had an iPhone. Just tell me how /
            to work the

MIKE   No, it's coded to me. My genetic – you won't be
            able to

BRIDGET   Please

MIKE   I'm on your side. I'm on your – trust me. I can tell
            you if he's alive, but not without –

            Not without that. So

BRIDGET   You promise you won't

MIKE   Please, I promise, just

            She hands him the device.

            Thank you.

            He backs away with it.

            Shall I switch her off?

VICTOR   Yes.

BRIDGET   What the / fuck

            BEEP. She is turned off.

They stand in silence beside the robot.

MIKE   I didn't enjoy that, Vic.

VICTOR   You aren't paid for the work to be easy, Mike.

MIKE   How many more of these do you want to run?

VICTOR   That was exciting, wasn't it? And you were right before. Under the correct circumstances, she can trust just fine. So / she's not completely

MIKE   Victor –

VICTOR   I think we're ready. Next one should be the last.

MIKE   I have to say, I don't – I don't feel – good. About what we're doing here.

VICTOR   Be serious.

MIKE   No, maybe she doesn't want this. Maybe she really

VICTOR   Didn't you see the way she snatched the Ops from your hand?

            How she ran when we threatened to turn her off?

            No. She may not know it, but she wants to live.

            I assure you, Mike. She does.

BEEP.

A new Bridget.

VICTOR   Bridget?

            Bridget, are you awake?

BRIDGET   Yes

VICTOR   Can you hear me?

BRIDGET   Yes

VICTOR   Good.

            Okay.

Now, you don't have to say anything, but I have some things to tell you.

Music.

My name's Victor. I work for a company called Edius. I'm afraid I have some bad news.

Music getting louder throughout the following so that eventually we cannot hear what he's saying.

Fifty years ago, our parent company, Kasner, had a lot of different operations. They had us, Edius. But they also had – I mean all kinds of things. Companies working on AI, data, understanding how people behaved online. They were also working on self-driving cars.

I don't know what the last thing you remember is. But I'm sorry to have to tell you that, unfortunately, you were struck by one of those cars, and shortly afterwards, you passed away.

We are watching them without being able to hear what is being said.

BRIDGET *mainly listens but once or twice she asks a question.*

Eventually:

5   Bridget has been awake for three-point-five seconds when she meets Victor. She trusts him immediately.

2   She has an uncanny – really, an almost uncanny sense that here is a person who understands what she needs, who will not lie to her.

3   The things he tells her are frightening, of course.

He tells her that this is the future.

4   He tells her that her body is dead, but she is alive.

5   He tells her that what happens next is up to her.

3	She has a choice to make. He says that he can turn her off, send her back into the dark, the nothing. Or –
4	She can live.

He goes out.

She is alone with the body.

5. THE PARTY

There is a party. DAVINA *needs air. She comes out to sit by herself.*

HARRY *finds her.*

HARRY   Darling, are you all right?

DAVINA   Yes

HARRY   You're not / feeling

DAVINA   I'm fine, Harry, don't fuss

HARRY   I've been looking for you.

DAVINA   Here I am

HARRY   Hiding away

DAVINA   Sitting down for five minutes / is not

HARRY   I was worried. You didn't have a funny turn or something?

DAVINA   No, no, for goodness' sake. It's just hot. I wanted to

HARRY   Hot?

DAVINA   Mm.

           Beat.

HARRY   You're lying.

DAVINA   Harry!

HARRY   You have a tell, it's a sort of eyebrow thing you do.

DAVINA   Oh, please.

HARRY   Go on. What's wrong?

           Beat. He sits with her.

           You always used to get nervous on your birthday, didn't you?

DAVINA   I'm not nervous.

HARRY   There was one party, wasn't there, when you were actually sick.

DAVINA   I don't think

HARRY   Yes, I remember. When you turned sixty

DAVINA   Fifty.

HARRY   Was it?

DAVINA   Yes

HARRY   I thought it was later, the time we rented that house. When Lizzy was finishing school and

DAVINA   No, no

HARRY   No?

DAVINA   No, it was my fiftieth, definitely, because I was wearing that very complicated dress / with the straps

HARRY   with the straps, yes, I remember it

DAVINA   And that's the one I wore for my fiftieth. We had the framed photo from the garden above the hall table

HARRY   Oh, yes

DAVINA   and – god

           I distinctly recall trying to kneel over the toilet because I just felt so, so sick, and that stupid dress, it wouldn't

HARRY   You know, you said for years it was food poisoning.

DAVINA   No, I didn't.

HARRY   Yes you did, and it's good to hear you admit –
          that's all – to hear you admit it was nerves.

DAVINA   Oh, shut up Harry, you're meant to be kind to me
          on my birthday

HARRY   I am! I will be

          I've written a lovely speech

DAVINA   Have you?

HARRY   Calling you all sorts of nice things

DAVINA   Have you really?

HARRY   Darling. What on earth have you got to be nervous
          about?

DAVINA   Nothing.

          I'm not.

          It's just…

          All those people.

HARRY   Ah.

DAVINA   And the caterers were late and

HARRY   Oh that was fine

DAVINA   And they're just a bit – I mean, they're not terribly
          attentive, are they

HARRY   Well

DAVINA   I touched Eliza's glass earlier and her champagne
          was, it was warm, so

HARRY   Was it really?

DAVINA   You don't believe me?

HARRY   No, I do, I do, but there's all those buckets / of ice

DAVINA   Yes, but they're refilling the glasses from the

HARRY   Don't give it another thought.

DAVINA   Harry

HARRY   No, darling, if it's worrying you, I'll deal with it.
           I want this to be perfect for you.

           Beat.

DAVINA   All those people.

HARRY   With their warm champagne? Don't worry about
           them

DAVINA   / No

HARRY   Everyone's having a / marvellous time

DAVINA   No, it's not that. It's

HARRY   What?

DAVINA   They're all looking at me.

           I'm so old.

HARRY   Oh, that

DAVINA   Eighty. It just sounds so

           Don't laugh

           My grandmother died when she was eighty, did
           you know that? Her strength, her mind, all –

           And I know I'm lucky, Harry, but it really does
           feel just –

           Too – too *old*

HARRY   Davina, you're beautiful

DAVINA   No

HARRY   So beautiful I could

DAVINA   Stop

HARRY   But it's true. *Age shall not wither her, nor custom
           stale her infinite variety.*

DAVINA   Is that what you're going to say in your speech?

HARRY   Yes, why not?

          'Ladies and gentlemen, my beautiful wife. My old, old, beautiful wife'

DAVINA   (*Laughing.*) Okay

HARRY   'Like a horse ready for the knacker's yard'

DAVINA   Well don't say that

HARRY   Who's writing this speech, you or me?

          DAVINA *is swallowed by the party.* HARRY *sees* VICTOR.

          You look like a man in need of a drink.

VICTOR   Oh. No

HARRY   Not looking for the bar?

VICTOR   Er

HARRY   I thought you might be lost. Because this part of the house is [*private.*]

          Beat.

          Can't be a friend of Davina's if you don't drink! Although you must be, because I don't think we've met. How do you know her?

VICTOR   I don't, actually. I mean I don't know [*this wife.*]

HARRY   Ha. Right, sorry. So how do you know me?

VICTOR   We've actually never met before.

          Beat.

HARRY   Oh

VICTOR   I'm sorry to impose. I wasn't really planning to – I saw the party, and then I was inside, and I just – I need to talk to you, and

HARRY   This is very unorthodox. Should I call security?

VICTOR   It won't take long.

          Beat.

HARRY   No, look, I'm sorry, but you can see that there's a
          party going on here, can't you? All these people,
          these trays of champagne, I mean, I don't just live
          like this. You understand that, don't you? I'm busy

VICTOR   Yes, of course, it's just – this is quite / urgent

HARRY   Well it's not the time. So let's go back outside, by
          all means have a drink on us, and then I think you
          should go

VICTOR   It's about Bridget.

          Beat.

HARRY   What?

VICTOR   Your first wife. I mean your – your late wife.

HARRY   Bridget.

VICTOR   Yes. I need to talk to you.

          It won't take long.

          Beat.

HARRY   All right.

VICTOR   Thank you, Mr Ingram. It's nice to meet you, by
          the way. My name's Victor – Victor Thomas.

          He offers his hand. HARRY doesn't accept.

          Right. Well.

          I'm here on behalf of my employer, Edius. We
          work across biochemistry, psychology and anti-
          senescence on some, if I do say so myself, really
          quite pioneering life-preservation technology.

          Actually, perhaps you've come across our work
          already?

HARRY   What do you mean?

VICTOR   Only that – you look very well. For your age. So
          does your wife.

HARRY   My wife?

VICTOR   It's her birthday, isn't it? Her / eightieth

HARRY   Sorry, I thought you said this was about / Bridget

VICTOR   Bridget, yes, sorry

           So: fifty years ago, you very generously gave
           permission for Bridget's brain to be / removed
           from her body

HARRY   What are you talking about?

VICTOR   and stored in a facility maintained by

HARRY   I gave permission?

VICTOR   Yes. Very generously. For her brain to be removed
           from her body, after her death – for which, many
           condolences – / and

HARRY   No I didn't.

VICTOR   What?

HARRY   I didn't do that, I didn't / do anything like that

VICTOR   Well I assure you, you did, or I / wouldn't

HARRY   Have you really come here to tell me that
           Bridget – that you have –

           That you've still got some *part* of her? Some
           piece of

VICTOR   Well

DAVINA   (*Off.*) Darling. Darling.

HARRY   That's my wife. Be quiet.

VICTOR   Mr Ingram, I assure you, there's / no need for

HARRY   Shhh

           DAVINA *enters.*

DAVINA   There you are, I was looking for you.

HARRY   Hello

DAVINA   Who's your friend?

VICTOR	I'm –
HARRY	Nobody. Old colleague. Just leaving, weren't you?
VICTOR	/ Erm
DAVINA	Oh, sorry you can't stay!

Harry, the waiters want to bring the Eton mess out – apparently they look tremendous but the heat isn't treating them well, so we thought better early than claggy. What do you say?

HARRY	Absolutely.
DAVINA	Good.

Awkward beat.

Are you coming back out?

HARRY	You go, I'm right behind you.

She leaves.

I'm walking you to the door, now. I don't want to see you again.

VICTOR	You'll change your mind.
HARRY	No.
VICTOR	I'll leave our details, just in case.
HARRY	Bridget's been dead fifty years. A lifetime.

Whatever you're selling, we don't want it.

VICTOR	I'm not selling anything. Mr Ingram –
HARRY	No, it's time for you to leave. I'm not going to change my mind.
VICTOR	I hope you're wrong. We need you. And you have the opportunity to be involved in something really tremendous here.
HARRY	For you?
VICTOR	For the human race.

He goes. HARRY *is alone.*

PAST BRIDGET *enters. She watches him. He sees her.*

HARRY   Bridget.

6. QUESTIONS AND ANSWERS

PAST BRIDGET *still onstage.* BRIDGET *approaches. Listens to her old body, its breath, its blood. Tries to remember how it felt.*

MIKE *is there.*

MIKE   Morning, Bridget

BRIDGET   Is it?

MIKE   Yes. Just after ten.

            You good?

            What you thinking about?

BRIDGET   Nothing

MIKE   Okay

            Well.

            Vic wanted me to get your questions, so.

BRIDGET   Again? We did it yesterday

MIKE   Yes, but you had a lot.

            And he thought there might be more things – unsettling you.

BRIDGET   Right

MIKE   Weighing on your mind. So

BRIDGET   Sure. Do you want me to just start asking things?

MIKE   Er

BRIDGET   So you can write them all down and not answer?

            Beat.

MIKE   Well

            Not answer *yet*. But when the time / comes

BRIDGET   Fine.

            I was thinking about my phone.

            Beat.

MIKE   / Your

BRIDGET   My mobile phone. Do you still have those? You must do.

MIKE   Do you want me to write that down?

BRIDGET   No, I didn't mean –

            I used to fall asleep reading – it was an awful habit, Harry hated it, but reading stuff online?

            And sometimes it's like I can still – feel it. My phone. In my hand. All those hours

            But I'm thinking, you know, fifty years. So it must be landfill or a museum or

MIKE   Is that – is this a / question

BRIDGET   And what about my heartbeat?

MIKE   What about it?

BRIDGET   I was thinking about that too, because I had one for like – thirty-five years – maybe longer, because –

            When does the heart start beating?

MIKE   A few weeks after conception. It's one of the / first

BRIDGET   Right. There you go: thirty-six years. Heartbeat. And now

            Quiet.

MIKE   Do you want me to write this down?

             Because it's not

             I don't really know how to make these a question.
             Sorry. Vic's better at this stuff. He / just

BRIDGET   Okay, Mike, no. Here's a question:

             How long can I survive without a heartbeat?

MIKE   Indefinitely.

BRIDGET   You don't have to write that down?

MIKE   No. This body will never tire, Bridget. It won't get
             old. It won't fall apart. That's not a –

             That's just a fact.

BRIDGET   How long can I *want* to survive without a
             heartbeat?

MIKE   Well, that's up to you.

BRIDGET   You love answering today, Mike!

             Okay, what about my parents? Any update on that?

             My husband?

             My sister?

             Anyone alive out there?

             Beat.

             Not going to answer those?

             Didn't think so.

MIKE   You heard what Victor said. It's a huge amount
             of change, of information. It's overwhelming. We
             don't want you to become –

BRIDGET   'Overwhelmed.'

MIKE   No.

             It's only been a few days. You have time. It's
             best – for you – if we just –

Take it slowly.

BRIDGET   Mm-hmm.

Yep.

Beat.

MIKE   Okay, Bridget.

I can see you're feeling

Delicate

Would you like to skip the questions today? We can move on. Do some more tests.

Beat.

If you're – feeling up to it.

BRIDGET   Actually, I do have a question.

MIKE   Yeah?

BRIDGET   What does it feel like?

MIKE   What does what feel like?

BRIDGET   In there. In your body. In –

MIKE   To me? What does it – what does my –

BRIDGET   Can you feel it beating?

He's slightly horrified. Something suddenly very inhuman about her.

MIKE   My

heart?

No.

No, not unless I –

I can take my pulse. But that's not the same.

BRIDGET   Huh.

I couldn't remember.

I already –

That's weird, right? Thirty-five years in my body. Breathing, sleeping, getting UTIs. And five days in this one. And already it's…

I can barely remember

how it felt.

+

VICTOR   I'm so glad to see you, Mr Ingram. I knew you'd change your mind.

HARRY   I'm not stopping. I have a car waiting outside.

VICTOR   All right. Let's speak in my office. I'll make it as quick as possible.

+

MIKE   Vic wanted us to do observations this morning. But if you're not feeling –

She shakes it off.

BRIDGET   No. I'm okay. Let's do them now.

+

HARRY   Let me get this straight.

You want to use Bridget's brain in your experiments. You want to make her some kind of lab rat, a test case, to see if, to see –

VICTOR   You already gave permission. You were paid.

HARRY   No, I received *compensation* – your company murdered my wife.

VICTOR   No fault proven, Mr Ingram. She was on her phone when she walked into the / path of

HARRY   No

VICTOR   We didn't owe you anything. But you chose to submit her remains to a complex and discreet trial, for which you were handsomely remunerated.

HARRY   My wife had just died. I loved Bridget, and she died.

VICTOR   Well, perhaps that's why you signed the forms.

HARRY   What?

VICTOR   Perhaps you wanted to believe that one day, you'd be able to see her, speak to her again. The finality of death, the cruelty of it – you rejected that finality, Mr Ingram. I think it's very brave.

            You wanted to believe that she could live again.

HARRY   What you're talking about isn't life. The things you're saying –

VICTOR   / Well

HARRY   No, no, no, I won't – I can't. I'm not leaving her here to be part of this

VICTOR   Mr Ingram

HARRY   Because surely it's, I must still be next of kin, right? Her wishes were very clear, so – so I can – yes, I withdraw my consent.

VICTOR   Harry

HARRY   No, no, whatever you're testing, that's your business, I might think you're all monsters but that's fine, go right ahead, but not –

            Not with her. All right? I withdraw – whatever consent you say I gave, I withdraw it. Henceforth.

VICTOR   I'm afraid that's not possible.

HARRY   I'm a powerful man. I / can

VICTOR   Oh I believe you. But I'm afraid we're beyond that stage now.

HARRY   Beyond –

            What do you mean, beyond?

            Beat.

            You came to my house. All the way to my house, looking for me.

VICTOR   You knew Bridget. You're the only living person
            who knew her. You can help us. You can verify –

HARRY   Verify?

VICTOR   There can be mistakes. It's a complicated process.
            One crossed wire and –

            She might feel like herself. But you'll know.
            You'll be able to confirm it.

HARRY   What have you done? What the hell have you done?

VICTOR   Harry, don't you want to see her?

            She's been asking for you.

                            +

MIKE   Okay, Bridget. We're going to look at some tests
            of muscle memory.

            Close your eyes for me. I want you to picture your
            kitchen.

            The kitchen you lived in before…

BRIDGET   Yes.

                            +

HARRY   It's not her.

VICTOR   How do you know?

HARRY   Her face – her voice, it – that's not her.

VICTOR   Oh, that. No, it wouldn't look like Bridget, the
            body wasn't made for her.

            Mike.

                            +

MIKE   Okay Bridget.

            We're interested in the things your body could do
            on instinct – your old body.

            We'd like to see you do them with this body.

BRIDGET   Er

MIKE   So I want you to walk me through – did you drink tea? Coffee?

BRIDGET   Both.

MIKE   So

           Picture yourself standing in your old kitchen.

           Now I'd like you to walk and talk me through making a cup of tea.

BRIDGET   Really?

MIKE   Please.

BRIDGET   Um.

           Okay.

           Well the door's here, behind me. There are these big windows as soon as you come into the room. We like –

           It's a small flat, but we liked the light, so.

           Hard water so. Water filter in the fridge. Which is here.

           Fill the kettle…

                              +

HARRY   I don't want to watch this.

VICTOR   Is it her, Harry? Is she the same?

HARRY   She can't be. This is like –

           It's a nightmare. I'm having a –

VICTOR   I can have Mike ask her things.

HARRY   No, no.

VICTOR   Anything you want.

                              +

BRIDGET   And then I'd sit down and drink my tea.

           Probably in the living room. That kitchen was
           always cold. Or I was cold.

           Harry always said I didn't wear enough / layers

HARRY   / layers, well you didn't, you'd go round the house
           in the middle of winter in a T-shirt, and put the
           bloody heating on.

BRIDGET   He said I should get a jumper before I put the
           heating on.

MIKE   What does that mean? 'Put the heating on'?

BRIDGET   Oh, it's like – hot water would go through all the
           pipes in the house. I think.

           To make it warmer.

MIKE   Wow

HARRY   It was very expensive.

BRIDGET   But if the house is cold, it's cold, you know? It
           doesn't matter what you're wearing.

HARRY   Bridget.

VICTOR   Ask her something.

HARRY   I can't.

VICTOR   Anything.

HARRY   I –

           Her –

           Her best holiday.

VICTOR   Mike, did you get that?

MIKE   Can I ask you more about your memories,
           Bridget?

BRIDGET   Vic usually does that, doesn't he?

MIKE   But while we're talking.

BRIDGET   Sure.

MIKE   Do you remember any holidays?

BRIDGET   Holidays? Yeah

MIKE   Do you remember your favourite?

BRIDGET   Oh, Florida.

VICTOR   Florida?

HARRY   We never went to –

BRIDGET   My sister was sick a long time when we were kids. Leukemia. It was awful. After she got better, Mum went crazy, she booked this huge holiday on credit cards. We'd never left the country before.

              My sister in the big mouse ears, you know? We were so.

              God. I don't want to talk about this, actually. Is that –

MIKE   That's fine. Anything more recent? With your husband maybe.

BRIDGET   Why?

MIKE   Just being nosy.

BRIDGET   Um

              Well my favourite was maybe

              Camber Sands

HARRY   Oh, god

VICTOR   You remember it?

BRIDGET   Not long after we got together

HARRY   Ask her where we stayed.

VICTOR   Mike.

MIKE   Where did you stay?

BRIDGET   This converted windmill. It was beautiful.

HARRY   No.

VICTOR   No?

HARRY   That was somewhere else. I thought it was –

BRIDGET   We had to get the bus. And it was so cold. The river by the windmill, all the marshland was frozen. So we just...

VICTOR   She's wrong?

HARRY   I don't know. I can't remember. I –

            Yes, it was cold. The windmill. Maybe.

BRIDGET   I swam even though it was winter. He thought I was crazy.

HARRY   You were freezing.

VICTOR   She's right?

HARRY   Does she wish we'd travelled more?

VICTOR   Mike.

MIKE   Do you wish you'd travelled more?

BRIDGET   Not really. We wanted to buy a flat. I wanted to get – I like cats. When we were renting, we couldn't –

HARRY   How many cats?

MIKE   How many?

BRIDGET   Oh, two at least.

            / One would get lonely.

HARRY   One would get lonely.

            Door slam.

            The scene breaks.

HARRY *is back home.*

DAVINA   Is that you, darling?

I just made a pot of coffee, do you want some?

Harry?

Gosh

HARRY   What

DAVINA   You're white as a sheet. Are you all right?

HARRY   Yes. Fine. I just have to

I have things to do.

DAVINA   Harry?

7. ROUGH JUSTICE

BRIDGET *is alone onstage.* CHORUS 2, 3, 4 *and* 5 *are on mics.*

2   A woman stands in a white room at what feels like the end of the world.

4   It has been, by her count, three hours since she was bundled from the testing room and left here.

5   No Vic. No Mike. Nobody.

Beat. Quiet.

2   It's a lot of time to think.

3   And wonder.

5   A lot of time to be alone.

4   Every night since she woke up in this body has seemed long, but somehow, these few hours have been the longest yet.

3	She's never felt more alone in her entire life.
	VICTOR *enters.*
VICTOR	Bridget. Well done.
5	Her creator.
	He shakes her by the hand.
VICTOR	You were marvellous. I know it hasn't been easy. But you have –
	Really. You've been fantastic.
4	The man she's trusted since she woke up in this place.
BRIDGET	What's going on?
VICTOR	We had good news today
	External confirmation of – of –
	That things are progressing. With you. With the project.
BRIDGET	What does that mean?
VICTOR	That you were observed and approved by an – a sort of expert
BRIDGET	Who?
VICTOR	This is good news, Bridget.
2	Who?
VICTOR	We can accelerate your development.
5	Who?
VICTOR	Take you upstairs to meet –
	Oh, lots of people. My boss. My boss's boss. Everyone's going to be very excited about you.
3	For a moment, she thinks of letting it go. Vic seems happy. And she trusts him.
4	She mostly trusts him.

2   But

BRIDGET   'observed'

VICTOR   What?

BRIDGET   You said 'observed and approved', what does /
           that

VICTOR   Oh. Well –

           Yes.

           They came in and – listened to you speak.
           Watched you moving around.

BRIDGET   The expert?

VICTOR   Yes.

BRIDGET   When I was with Mike?

           Someone was watching me when I was with Mike?

           When he made me do all that weird stuff

5   She's clever. That's why he chose her.

VICTOR   You're in a professional setting. You know we
           keep you under close observation – for your own
           good. You know that.

BRIDGET   Right.

VICTOR   / Don't be –

BRIDGET   But a test like that, I don't know what it could
           have been measuring. I really don't / understand
           what they

VICTOR   Okay. Fine.

4   The room is windowless. The door is sealed.

3   Why is she looking at the door? She trusts Victor.

VICTOR   I didn't want to tell you like this, but –

           You're right. It was an unusual test.

5	He chose this cleverness. Perhaps he thought it would make things easier.
VICTOR	The expert was someone who knew you, in your old life.
BRIDGET/CHORUS	Who?
	Beat.
VICTOR	Your husband. Harry.
BRIDGET	He's alive?
VICTOR	Yes, he's alive.
	She's overwhelmed. Covers her face with her hands.
	I thought you'd be pleased.
	Bridget?
BRIDGET	(*Muffled.*) I am.
	A long beat.
2	The silence stretches.
4	If she's trying to cry, she won't be able to.
2	The body is not equipped.
3	The people who made it saw no benefit in crying.
VICTOR	Bridget?
BRIDGET	I need to get out. I need to see him
VICTOR	No
BRIDGET	What do you mean, no?
VICTOR	He's gone. He's left
BRIDGET	He left me here? He / wouldn't
VICTOR	Calm down. There's no need to
BRIDGET	No need? My husband came here, and saw me like this, saw me

VICTOR	Bridget, this is good. This is good news. Harry said you were the same.
BRIDGET	Of course I'm the same
VICTOR	He knew it was you. He recognised you. Bridget, you don't understand how momentous this is – you're the same! You are Bridget!
BRIDGET	I know I'm fucking Bridget!
5	A breath
3	In a manner of speaking
4	Before the doubt sets in.
BRIDGET	You thought I might / not be me?
VICTOR	Things can go wrong. Mistakes can be made. One crossed wire and
BRIDGET	And what? What are you saying? Suddenly I want to go round punching old ladies
VICTOR	Bridget
BRIDGET	'She never punched old ladies when she was alive'
VICTOR	Nothing so dramatic. Just
BRIDGET	You're serious, aren't you?

There's a chance I might not be / the same? |
| VICTOR | No

Just a small – a very small |
BRIDGET	Victor
VICTOR	You have no organic tissue. You are a computer program, a brilliant, a very complicated program, based on a scan of your own brain – it's / possible something could
BRIDGET	Stop, stop
2	But too late

4	She can sense the thought lodging itself inside her
3	If she was human, she'd probably feel sick
BRIDGET	Let me out of this room you mad fucking bastard
VICTOR	Bridget
	She beats on the walls.
BRIDGET	Harry! Harry!
VICTOR	For god's sake, calm down
BRIDGET	Harry, somebody, please
VICTOR	Stop that
BRIDGET	Get me out of here please
VICTOR	You haven't acted like this since the beginning
BRIDGET	Since
	What are you talking about?
VICTOR	Nothing.
BRIDGET	I do
	I have always done
	Exactly as you've asked me to.
VICTOR	I know, I'm very grateful.
3	The room is windowless. The door is sealed.
4	Why is he looking at the door? It's just Bridget.
BRIDGET	What happened in the beginning, Victor?
VICTOR	Just what you remember. I woke you up.
BRIDGET	So what did you mean?
VICTOR	I misspoke.
BRIDGET	Yeah, I bet you did.

4	There are cameras in here, but nobody's watching.
5	He sent Mike out to get a bottle of champagne.
2	A toast. He thought the three of them would –
BRIDGET	Victor, what aren't you telling me?
5	He chose this cleverness
BRIDGET	Are there things I don't remember?
3	And Victor is suddenly, keenly aware of his heart beating
4	How fragile it is
BRIDGET	Are there things you haven't told me?
VICTOR	I
2	He's afraid of her. Afraid of his own creation.
VICTOR	No
BRIDGET	Things I've forgotten
VICTOR	No
BRIDGET	That you've made me forget
VICTOR	Bridget, please
3	*by the dim and yellow light of the moon, as it forced its way through the window shutters, I beheld the wretch—the miserable monster whom I had created*
BRIDGET	I'm a program, that's what you said. So you've been changing things. Rewriting. Deleting. Haven't you? Don't speak. I can see in your face –
VICTOR	I had to.
BRIDGET	I said don't speak

3	*No mortal could support the horror of that countenance. A mummy again endued with animation could not be so hideous as that wretch*
BRIDGET	I'm trying to think
2	*Frankenstein* was based on real science
VICTOR	Bridget please. Let me explain
2	what seemed like science at the time
BRIDGET	I don't want to listen to you any more
4	Galvanism. Electrodes on a dead frog
5	Watching its legs twitch
VICTOR	We didn't delete anything. Not as such.
	There were some
	There were mistakes
3	And George Foster
VICTOR	We – we had to start over.
3	Lifeless
VICTOR	When things got difficult, we had to start again.
2	Dead George Foster, twitching on the slab.
BRIDGET	You erased me.
VICTOR	Don't be so melodramatic
BRIDGET	How many times?
VICTOR	I don't
	I don't know.
BRIDGET	Until – what?
	Until I was happy?
	Until I trusted you.

2   George Foster was hanged because he'd murdered
           his wife and child.

           He drowned them, both of them, in a river. And
           then a scientist made Foster's lifeless body dance,
           for an audience of great men.

3   This is the story of progress: horror, with a grain
           inside it.

4   A small, hard grain, that is the future.

BRIDGET   I have to get out of here.

VICTOR   Bridget

BRIDGET   No, I have to get / out of here

VICTOR   Please

BRIDGET   LET ME OUT. LET ME OUT. LET ME OUT.

           Slamming against the door.

VICTOR   Stop that, you'll hurt yourself

BRIDGET   I don't feel it, I don't feel anything

VICTOR   I've had enough of this. I will turn you off if you
           don't stop

BRIDGET   Let me go

VICTOR   I can't

BRIDGET   Let me go!

VICTOR   You're being ridiculous, stop this, fucking stop.

           Even if you could get through that door, there is
           another behind it, and another door behind that
           one. This is a secure facility. Keycodes, / failsafes,

BRIDGET   So give me them

VICTOR   Retina scans. Bridget, you aren't getting out of
           here unless I let you.

           And I'm not going to let you. Okay?

BRIDGET   Retina scans.

VICTOR   What?

           What are you doing?

           Bridget.

           She pulls out his eye.

           Interval.

ACT TWO

1. THE HOUSEGUEST

BRIDGET *and* MIKE *onstage. Waiting.*

She is very still. He is making some kind of annoying repetitive motion. Rolling something across the table? It gets louder and louder.

BRIDGET   Stop that.

                        He flinches. Stops.

MIKE   Sorry.

                        He's scared of her.

                        Silence.

                        What are you thinking?

BRIDGET   Nothing.

                        She was his wife, wasn't she? The woman who let us in.

                        He married again.

MIKE   Well, you were gone a long time.

BRIDGET   No, I just meant –

                        You know.

                        They might not want me to stay.

                        Beat.

                        HARRY *in the doorway. They look at each other.*

                        Harry.

Cut to:

HARRY	This is the room. It's en suite.
BRIDGET	Right.
HARRY	Towels. Shower gel. It's all
BRIDGET	Thanks.

Beat.

Can you just – sorry. Can you look at me, please?

I know it's weird, and hard, but –

Thank you.

For taking me in.

HARRY   What else could I do?

Beat. Held.

You should get some sleep. It's been a long

A strange

Anyway.

BRIDGET   Yes. Okay.

See you in the morning.

Cut to:

HARRY	She has to go.
DAVINA	I'm sorry?
HARRY	It's too much

Too

Strange, it's

We made a mistake.

DAVINA   Harry

HARRY   Don't, don't look at me like that, like I'm some /
               sort of

DAVINA   I'm not looking at you in any / particular

HARRY   I can't

               I just

               Can't go through with it. And I know we discussed
               it, we agreed that it's / not

DAVINA   It's not her fault

HARRY   I know, and she didn't ask for any

DAVINA   Right

HARRY   But I –

               Can't. Davina, it's impossible. Imagine it was you

DAVINA   Me? In the

HARRY   No. No! If you were me, and somebody you knew
               fifty years ago, half a century, somebody you
               loved

DAVINA   I know it's hard, Harry, but you're / being
               completely

HARRY   Sssh.

               Keep your voice down. I don't want her to hear.

DAVINA   (*Quieter.*) Oh.

               Oh no, of course.

               Nothing uncomfortable, no nasty scenes, we can
               just – what? Call them up, pop to the shops, leave
               the door open, let those laboratory men sweep her
               into a black bag / and

HARRY   I'm not saying that!

DAVINA   If we don't protect her, they will kill her. That's
               what he said, that man. If we don't keep her here,
               if they take her back to the lab, she will be killed.

HARRY   But she isn't really alive.

            Shocked beat.

DAVINA   Harry.

            We gave our word.

HARRY   I know. / But

DAVINA   And what if it *was* me?

HARRY   What?

DAVINA   If it was me, back from the –

            Upstairs. Inside the –

            Me. In there.

HARRY   Don't be absurd. That's not –

            You're my wife.

DAVINA   Yes. So was she.

            Long beat.

HARRY   Okay.

DAVINA   Okay?

HARRY   You're right. I'm sorry.

DAVINA   Harry.

HARRY   But I need, I do need –

            Space.

            Beat.

DAVINA   How much space?

HARRY   A day, two, I don't know, just

            Get away. Clear my head.

            You understand, don't you?

            That I need –

            Hard cut.

2. A NEW DAY

It's early morning. DAVINA *enters the kitchen to find*
BRIDGET *already there.*

DAVINA   Oh!

           Bridget. Good morning. You're

           Up early.

           You startled me.

           Did

           Did you sleep all right?

BRIDGET   I don't.

DAVINA   I'm sorry?

BRIDGET   I don't sleep. I can't.

DAVINA   Goodness, really?

           Beat.

BRIDGET   Is Harry

DAVINA   He, er

           Yes, he's had to go out. Just for a

           There's a trip. Some old friends. He was going to
           miss it, but I said

           You know

           Go! Enjoy yourself! So, it's –

           It's just us for a bit. Sorry.

BRIDGET   Anyone I know?

DAVINA   Excuse me?

BRIDGET   You said 'old friends'. Is it anyone

DAVINA   Oh

No. No.

Beat.

Breakfast!

Would you like anything? I'm having

She checks a screen. Annoyed.

Hm, porridge apparently, even though I'd rather have Greek yogurt.

Would you like some? We've got honey, brown sugar, bananas…

BRIDGET   Why?

DAVINA   Why what?

BRIDGET   Why can't you have what you want?

DAVINA   Oh

I can. But apparently I need the fibre. It's a sort of –

Yes, I suppose you've missed all this.

I have a chip, here, that monitors my – well, most things

Beat.

BRIDGET   Can I see?

DAVINA   Er

All right.

She lifts her jaw. BRIDGET *looks.*

Not much *to* see, I'm afraid. Just an old scar.

BRIDGET   Does everyone have these?

DAVINA   Most people.

BRIDGET   Weird.

DAVINA   Is it?

So, what about that porridge? Or – or whatever you like. Toast, or

BRIDGET   No, there's no point.

DAVINA   You can't…?

BRIDGET   I can taste.

But

No. I don't get hungry.

DAVINA   Gosh. Okay. Well.

Why don't I make two bowls? And then you can just see. What you feel like.

BRIDGET   Okay. Thanks.

Quiet. A little awkward. DAVINA *works,* BRIDGET *watches her. A woman at home in her own space. She puts two bowls of porridge on the table, eats one.*

PAST BRIDGET *sits at the table. She eats the other bowl. She lip-syncs to* BRIDGET*'s voice. It should feel ghostly. Alienated.*

BRIDGET   You have a beautiful home.

DAVINA   Thank you.

BRIDGET   I'm

I appreciate it.

Letting me stay.

DAVINA   No, of course. Of course.

You're

family.

Beat.

BRIDGET   Thank you.

DAVINA   I've actually always been curious to meet you.

BRIDGET   Really?

DAVINA   He used to

            Anyway. I should really

            DAVINA *stands.* PAST BRIDGET *leaves.*
            BRIDGET *retakes her place.*

            I need to get on.

            Will you be all right here by yourself?

            I can put a film on for you, or

            Sorry, what a ridiculous thing to say. You're not
            a child

BRIDGET   No, no, I

            Can I come?

DAVINA   Can / you

BRIDGET   Can I come with you? On whatever you're

            Sorry, I know that's weird, I just

            I've been alone so much and it's – awful –
            so I thought

            But it's fine, obviously. I know that would be –

            Sorry. It's fine.

            Beat.

Cut to:

BRIDGET   It's lovely.

DAVINA   Well, it keeps me busy

BRIDGET   The roses are – so –

DAVINA   Thanks. It was just a lawn when we moved in

BRIDGET   Really?

DAVINA   Everything you see was my

Anyway, it's just killing time really

Retirement!

BRIDGET   Can I ask you – something that might / sound

DAVINA   Of course

BRIDGET   What time of year is it?

DAVINA   Now? You don't – they didn't tell you?

May.

BRIDGET   Oh.

DAVINA   Is that what you expected?

Or… does it feel different to how you remember?

BRIDGET   Everything feels different.

DAVINA   Right.

BRIDGET   It's a lovely garden.

DAVINA   Thanks.

BRIDGET   And – out there – I mean, are we –

Cut to:

DAVINA   Most basic amenities. Shops. Healthcare. Exercise studio.

BRIDGET   Sure

DAVINA   Food-wise it's okay. Couple of cafés, a decent Italian, a not-very-good Thai…

BRIDGET   It's bigger than I thought

DAVINA   Did I make it sound small?

BRIDGET   I don't know. Yeah. Like Center Parcs

DAVINA   I don't think I ever went to one of those.

BRIDGET   But this is more like a big village

DAVINA   I suppose it's just too familiar, I take it for granted.
            But

            I was in London for forty-nine years, Bridget.
            I mean, the food

BRIDGET   Yeah

DAVINA   The compound just doesn't compare.

            It can't. And I mean, obviously there are other
            advantages. Ease, you know.

            Security.

BRIDGET   Right

DAVINA   Do you want to get a coffee or something while
            I go to my exercise class?

BRIDGET   Er

Cut to:

DAVINA *does a HIIT class to something like 'Freed from
Desire' by GALA. It's really intense.* BRIDGET *watches.*

Cut to:

DAVINA *at a dressing table. She is applying a cream.*

DAVINA   Don't judge me. You've never been old.

BRIDGET   You're not old.

DAVINA   That's kind, Bridget, but I just turned eighty.

BRIDGET   Wow.

            Sorry

            I mean, er

            DAVINA *laughs.*

DAVINA   It's okay.

BRIDGET   You don't look it, either of you. I did the maths.
            I was expecting

            You know

DAVINA   A little old man

BRIDGET   Yeah

DAVINA   He did look old to you, though? He must have

BRIDGET   Well

DAVINA   Don't tell me you didn't notice the difference
            because I won't believe you

BRIDGET   To be honest it was

            Too weird.

            [*To notice.*]

            Beat.

            But you don't look like a

            Like eighty-year-olds used to look.

DAVINA   Yes. There are very good

            There are injections. Things like that. People
            stay healthier for longer. But, you know. It's not
            indefinite.

BRIDGET   Can I ask what that is?

DAVINA   Oh – eye serum. It sort of regenerates the

            Under here – very thin skin under the eyes

BRIDGET   Can I try?

DAVINA   Er

            Yes. All right

            DAVINA *puts the serum on the back of*
            BRIDGET*'s hand.*

BRIDGET   Like this?

DAVINA   Pat it in. Like this. Gently.

BRIDGET   I never did this when I was alive

DAVINA   Really?

BRIDGET   I moisturised, but I wasn't

DAVINA   No, well. I didn't start until I was

            Mid-, late thirties

BRIDGET   Mm.

            Well, I guess, now, I'm

            Kind of glad I never bothered.

DAVINA   You've got beautiful skin.

            Can I…?

BRIDGET   Sure.

            DAVINA *applies the serum to* BRIDGET*'s face.*

            What does it feel like?

DAVINA   Just – skin. Like it's real.

3. DINNER FOR THREE

HARRY *is there.*

HARRY   Right.

            I'm back

DAVINA   Harry

HARRY   Hi, both of you

            Wow

            sitting here together. Which is

            Great, obviously, that's great

            I'm er

God, this is so

Fucking

Strange. Isn't it?

So, anyway, Davina – this is / Bridget

DAVINA   Yes, I / know

HARRY   No I know you know but it's, sorry, I need to / do it properly

DAVINA   We've met, Harry.

Do you think we just sat in silence waiting for you to get back?

HARRY   Ha

No, sorry, right – I do understand that you're

But can I just?

I should say. I feel I should say.

Bridget. We are going to – we are going to find a way to sort this out. I know there's got to be a plan, there's got to be legal things, all that, but I just

I should have said. Yesterday. And I

That was my failure. That I didn't. But.

Yes. Because we're going to have to find a way through it, aren't we? Otherwise we'll all go mad, so, / there we are

BRIDGET   Yes, okay, thank you.

Beat. Tense. Is this the first moment he realises she's angry? How familiar is it?

The trip was good for you, then. Cleared your mind.

HARRY   Trip?

BRIDGET   Davina told me. Some trip with friends. What was it?

DAVINA   / Fishing

HARRY   Golf

             Beat.

             Golf and fishing. It was a – you know.

BRIDGET   Right.

             Well.

             Well done for getting through it. Can't have been easy.

DAVINA   Do you know what? I might go and start dinner. Leave you two to talk.

HARRY   No, please don't

             I mean

             I'll cook. I've brought

DAVINA   Okay

BRIDGET   Can I just say one thing?

             And I'm not saying that this is what happened.

             PAST BRIDGET *enters.* HARRY *sees her. He is seeing, remembering Bridget as she was.*

BRIDGET(S)   But I'm saying that –

PAST BRIDGET   If you were freaked out, and you needed some space, I would understand.

             I would understand that, Harry.

             I mean, this whole thing is

HARRY   Crazy

PAST BRIDGET   I know

HARRY   Like a nightmare

PAST BRIDGET   I know. I agree.

             And you're entitled to…

             But I won't be lied to. Or treated like a child. Because

I may not look the same. But give me some credit, Harry, as someone who knows you, who's known you for –

I mean, honestly, it's almost reassuring. You have always, literally always disappeared when things get –

Not in a bad way. But I mean, even after we got engaged –

You asked, and I said yes, and then two days later it was

Vroom, out the door, that walking trip, do you remember?

HARRY   God.

PAST BRIDGET   Yeah, you walked from – it must have been fifteen miles, you had to get the train back, and you'd worn the wrong / shoes and

HARRY   I'd completely forgotten that

PAST BRIDGET   Right. So.

Were you on a golf-fishing trip?

HARRY   No.

PAST BRIDGET   Okay then.

Beat.

DAVINA   What did you do?

HARRY   I drove around. Um. And then I just

DAVINA   Walked.

HARRY   Yes.

DAVINA *starts laughing.*

What?

DAVINA   Sorry. It just struck me as – funny.

Two wives.

Not really, but.

BRIDGET *laughs too. Both* BRIDGETS? *A sense of release. Maybe not for* HARRY, *who doesn't join in.*

PAST BRIDGET   Harry, now that you're back, I have a question.

HARRY   Of course. You must have – a lot of them

PAST BRIDGET   Yeah.

My sister. They wouldn't tell me. Is she alive, or

Beat.

HARRY   Er

No. I'm sorry Bridget. She's –

She died, I think.

PAST BRIDGET *leaves.* BRIDGET *retakes her place.*

BRIDGET   Right.

Do you know how?

HARRY *and* DAVINA *look at each other.*

HARRY   No. I just – I heard that she

BRIDGET   Okay. I might. If you don't mind – I might just

DAVINA   Of course

HARRY *and* DAVINA *are alone. They look at each other.*

HARRY   Did you say anything to her?

About

DAVINA   No. I didn't know how

Did you?

HARRY   No.

Beat. Then we cut into –

4. BACK TO THE DRAWING BOARD

We are in the lab again.

VICTOR   What about your childhood? Do you remember
                that?

ELOISE   Childhood?

                Yes. I remember everything

VICTOR   Do you?

ELOISE   I remember the

                The fields I used to cross to get to school

                Going home in the winter, it would be nearly dark

                Crows calling over our heads, and

                My mum, my brothers, just the four of us

                I remember my first night away. How much I cried

                Yes, I remember my childhood very clearly.

VICTOR   No blank spaces?

ELOISE   Oh, no

VICTOR   And you know what's happening to you?

ELOISE   Of course. I was dying in, what was it? 2068. And
                I was on the Edius Health Programme. I became a
                platinum member, which came with the option, the
                experimental

VICTOR   Yes

ELOISE   But I didn't think it would actually

VICTOR   No, well, the technology's still in development

ELOISE   It's amazing.

                MIKE *is there.*

MIKE   What's going on?

ELOISE   Oh, hello

MIKE   Victor, what / the hell are you

ELOISE   / Who's this?

VICTOR   Turn off please, Angela

MIKE   Angela?

ANGELA   (*Voice-over.*) Turning off

             The ROBOT *shuts down. Awkward beat.*

MIKE   You're working with Angela?

VICTOR   You've been away

MIKE   I've been sleeping. It's eight-thirty a.m. And you
             should, you're supposed to be, I mean, why / are
             you here

VICTOR   I'm fine, Mike

MIKE   Fine? She pulled out / your

VICTOR   Sssssh. Please.

             He gestures to Angela.

MIKE   Send her on a break then

VICTOR   I decide when we break. This is *my* –

             Beat. Tense.

             Five minutes

MIKE   Ten.

VICTOR   Fine. Let's take ten please, Angela.

ANGELA   (*Voice-over.*) …All right. See you

             Beat. MIKE *and* VICTOR *look at each other.*

MIKE   So?

VICTOR   So what? I've been treated. I've recovered

MIKE   You're acting like nothing happened

VICTOR   I'd have thought that's what you wanted. You're
           the one who helped her escape. Edius property.
           Incredibly secret, incredibly / expensive

MIKE   I said I was / sorry

VICTOR   You said you were scared

MIKE   She'd pulled out your eye!

VICTOR   So she takes you hostage, fine, could happen to
           anyone

           Then you get back here, and – what?

           Do you go rushing straight upstairs to tell them
           everything, like a good little boy?

           No, of course not. Because you knew a mess like
           this would mean our jobs.

           Didn't you?

           And that's why we have to – push on. We have no
           choice.

MIKE   You were running uploads

VICTOR   Yes.

MIKE   Back to the drawing board – Vic, that's insane

VICTOR   What's the alternative?

MIKE   I don't know, anything. Stop

VICTOR   Stop?

MIKE   We could get a transfer. Go / back to bionics, or

VICTOR   We brought a woman back from the dead.

           From the dead, Mike.

           Fifty years ago. Crossing a road. And suddenly all
           her thoughts, memories, everything that made her
           who she was, it was all

           He clicks his fingers.

           Gone.

A complicated – an infinitely complicated accrual of infinitely delicate – joys. And fears. Memories. Preferences. All that we are. And we brought it back.

How can we stop now? We're so

unbelievably

close.

MIKE   Close to what?

VICTOR   To –

To –

He stops himself. Beat.

MIKE   To what, Victor? Getting your other eye pulled out?

VICTOR   All right, fine. Let's say we do stop. Go back to bionics.

How long have we got until she turns back up? Because Harry Ingram's died, or got sick of having his dead wife in the spare room – how long till something goes wrong?

And then what? She pops up here, at the reception desk, asking for us? She goes to the press?

She is a time bomb. And we have to get ahead of that bomb going off.

There's only one way to do that. Nothing but victory is going to fix this mess.

MIKE   That's why you were doing / more

VICTOR   Yes. Bridget's proof of concept – it worked with her, we can make it work with somebody else. And when we do, we're free. We can go upstairs and confess the whole thing.

Once we have our breakthrough, once they know everything we've achieved, everything we've made possible, no one's going to mind a few…

MIKE   Mistakes.

VICTOR   Exactly.

MIKE   So we just leave her there?

VICTOR   For now, yes.

            What other option do we have? Unless you're
            suggesting we switch her off while she's there. In
            the house. I mean, imagine the headlines

            'Evil scientists brought my wife back from the
            dead, then killed her / again'

MIKE   Don't

VICTOR   We leave her there and get back to work. Right?

MIKE   I don't know.

VICTOR   You're the one who let her go, Mike. You need a
            win just as much as I do.

            Maybe more.

MIKE   Yes.

            You

            You're right. Course you are. We have to keep
            going.

VICTOR   Good man.

            Bridget gave us so much trouble anyway. There's
            got to be plenty that are more – biddable. Trusting.
            More grateful for

            BEEP.

ELOISE   Towards the end I was in a bed for months and
            months and months. Nothing worked. And
            I dreamt about this. Being able to

VICTOR   Yes

ELOISE   I was a dancer, when I was young. And I wanted,
            before I died, all I really wanted was

This. To be able to move again, without pain

To be able to

Move

VICTOR   Try moving now.

Long beat. The ROBOT *does not move.*

Eloise?

ELOISE   I

I'm trying

Please

5. ANCIENT HISTORY

'Freed from Desire' by GALA plays.

DAVINA *does her HIIT class.*

Meanwhile – PAST BRIDGET *in the kitchen, chopping an onion.*

DAVINA *still going. Eventually she is so tired she can no longer stand. She sits on the floor. She lies down.*

PAST BRIDGET *cannot see* DAVINA. *She keeps cooking.*

BRIDGET *is watching her.*

PAST BRIDGET   Harry?

He enters.

Have you got a cheese grater? Sorry, I couldn't find

HARRY   Oh, yes.

Hang on

PAST BRIDGET   Thank god, I thought maybe they didn't exist any more

HARRY   Of course they exist. You thought cheese graters were

PAST BRIDGET   I don't know, I thought it might all be – space graters, or – thanks

HARRY   What are you doing?

PAST BRIDGET   What's it look like?

HARRY   No, yes, sorry, I just thought you didn't really eat

PAST BRIDGET   It's not for me. I wanted to do something for you – you and Davina

HARRY   Oh. That's very kind

PAST BRIDGET   It's just pasta, Harry

He touches the chip in his neck. Doubtful.

HARRY   Is it?

PAST BRIDGET   What's wrong with pasta?

HARRY   Nothing

PAST BRIDGET   Is this your – Davina told me, you all have these, what you can eat and when you can eat it

HARRY   No, it'll be lovely, I'm sure. We just

Don't really ever eat carbs on a weekday.

She stops chopping.

PAST BRIDGET   Right. Shall I stop? / Because I thought it might be nice but if it's going to stress you out

HARRY   No, please don't, the stupid chip, it's not

Stop.

It's the courgette pasta, right? I remember it.

PAST BRIDGET   Yes.

HARRY   Go on, please. It will be delicious.

We'll just – fast over the weekend.

A look. He's joking.

Do they laugh? Something nice. Some warmth.

Companionable silence for a bit. She chops.

I'm sorry, Bridget.

PAST BRIDGET   Why?

HARRY   I just, I must seem. Different

PAST BRIDGET   Don't. I mean look at me, I'm completely

HARRY   You're not

PAST BRIDGET   No

HARRY   You're the same.

PAST BRIDGET   Harry, don't be ridiculous, I don't / look
anything like

HARRY   I'm not. Really. You

The way you hold yourself, it's, somehow

Exactly the same.

Beat.

PAST BRIDGET   The same as what?

HARRY   What do you mean?

PAST BRIDGET   I just

I worry it's not – how I remember. I feel so
different. And you

I don't know.

What was I like?

HARRY   What were you like? God, I don't know, what's
anybody like?

PAST BRIDGET   Please.

Beat.

HARRY   Direct? Always very direct. Very certain.
               Compared to me anyway. I used to think, you
               always knew what the right thing to do was, right
               away, you'd always have the answer, and I missed
               it, I really missed it for a long time after you

               He can't say it. Beat.

               You were an aggressive tidier.

               But it was funny because you were so good at
               all these things, but if there was something you
               couldn't do, like some household, or

               I don't know
               you had a terrible sense of direction and you'd
               suddenly seem to me like a little kid, like a seven-
               year-old, very trusting, and I liked
               I liked to think
               I was the only one who got to see that.
               Erm.

               You weren't afraid of other people's emotions,
               which was

               I don't know. Does that help at all?

PAST BRIDGET   I think so.

               A long beat.

HARRY   What about me?

PAST BRIDGET   What about you?

HARRY   What was I like?

PAST BRIDGET   Exactly the same.

HARRY   No.

PAST BRIDGET   Yes, of course

HARRY   The same as what? What do you

               What was I

PAST BRIDGET   Well, you were always

               Okay. You

You made me feel

Centred, I guess? I know that sounds really

But I always felt kind of, restless, and like I was focused on the next thing, on what I wanted our life to look like, on the future, and you were really good at just um

Being 'in the moment'. Do people still say that?

HARRY   Bridget, go on. Please.

PAST BRIDGET   You were so

Generous? If that's not a weird thing to say. With your time, your – everything. You always had time for people. You made them feel safe. You were very

Open. To the world. Very

Sorry, I just. I can't get used to

It's been a week, ten days since I said goodbye to you and

HARRY   No

PAST BRIDGET   Yes, of course. For me. No time at all between that day, crossing the road, and

Waking up in the lab.

HARRY   I hadn't thought.

God. That's so

PAST BRIDGET   Yeah. It is.

                 Beat.

HARRY   You must remember it all so clearly.

                 Our life. To me it feels

PAST BRIDGET   Yeah

HARRY   So, can you

                 I don't know

What's something we did last month? To you. Last month, to you

PAST BRIDGET   I don't

HARRY   Anything

PAST BRIDGET   Well. Your birthday

HARRY   God. Of course. Because

PAST BRIDGET   Your thirty-eighth

HARRY   What did we do?

PAST BRIDGET   Not much. You didn't want to do anything big. We just

Got coffee. Went round the record shop

And I cooked

I made a sort of – overcomplicated soufflé. Johnny and Mark came for dinner, and Mark always did such fiddly things that I felt like I should make an effort, do you know what I mean?

Oh god, Johnny and Mark

What happened to them? Are they alive?

HARRY   Ah.

PAST BRIDGET   Ah? What does that mean, 'ah'?

HARRY   There are just

Some things I've been meaning to tell you.

+

BRIDGET   Davina?

God

DAVINA   I'm fine

BRIDGET   Are you?

DAVINA   Yes, sorry, I'm

BRIDGET   When I saw you lying there, I thought

DAVINA   No, no. Not dead yet

            Sorry, I was just. Tired. And then I –

BRIDGET   It's your house. If you want to lie on the floor, / it's

DAVINA   Thanks. You won't remember. I mean, it must
            seem strange

BRIDGET   Lying on the floor?

DAVINA   Being tired, being

            You don't feel pain any more, do you? Or
            exhaustion, or

BRIDGET   No, but I remember how it feels

DAVINA   Really? I would have thought it was difficult. Like
            trying to remember feeling warm when you're
            cold, or cold when / you're hot, or

BRIDGET   No

            You're right. I don't remember.

                            +

PAST BRIDGET   Matt and Soph?

HARRY   No

PAST BRIDGET   Phoebe?

HARRY   No

PAST BRIDGET   Aki?

HARRY   No

PAST BRIDGET   Lucas?

HARRY   Lucas? I can't

            I can't remember / who

PAST BRIDGET   We worked with him. When we met, he was
                head of / Key Stage Three at

HARRY   Oh god. With the glasses.

PAST BRIDGET   He was French

HARRY   He was French and he taught French.

PAST BRIDGET   Yeah

HARRY   I'd completely forgotten about him. Lucas. Wow.

PAST BRIDGET   So…

     Beat.

HARRY   No.

          No, I don't – I wouldn't have thought –

          Maybe?

          But

          Probably not.

PAST BRIDGET   Right.

          Did anyone

          Anyone else

          Is *anyone* I knew still alive?

          Long pause.

HARRY   I'm sorry, Bridget.

          Like I said: it was a bad time.

          Awful.

          You can't imagine.

PAST BRIDGET   But you're okay.

HARRY   What?

PAST BRIDGET   You and Davina. You're

                              +

DAVINA   I do actually feel

          Sometimes

          Jealous.

BRIDGET   Of me?

DAVINA   Is that so strange?

BRIDGET   I just don't understand why you would be.

DAVINA   Oh come on, Bridget. You can't imagine?

BRIDGET   Well

DAVINA   You're at the start. You're at the very start of it all, and I am –

            I am at the end.

            I'm old, Bridget. Much older than I look, and much, much older than I feel. And I will die. I might get ten, twenty more years, but I am –

            In the final act.

            And you have something beyond value. Of course I'm jealous.

BRIDGET   Beyond value?

DAVINA   To live. Yes. Something that money can't buy.

            What?

BRIDGET   Nothing. I just. I don't think that this –

            The body.

            I don't think it is

            'Something that money can't buy.'

                              +

HARRY   We were lucky, I guess.

PAST BRIDGET   That's the answer? Luck?

HARRY   A lot of luck. A lot / of

PAST BRIDGET   Right

HARRY   I try not to stir up the past too much – at my age, it's

PAST BRIDGET   No, sure

HARRY   But I know I've been lucky. Except for what
             happened with you.

             Losing you. Like that.

PAST BRIDGET   It was sudden.

HARRY   It was awful, Bridget. And everything

             Everything went with you. Our life. Everything
             we'd planned, everything we'd thought we might

PAST BRIDGET   Yeah

HARRY   The future – and the past, too, everything we'd
             done together

             Because there was no one who remembered it,
             remembered all our

             History

             Until now.

             Will you tell me more?

             More things you remember, more

PAST BRIDGET   Oh

HARRY   Anything. Anything you

PAST BRIDGET   I don't know, I can't

HARRY   Anything at all

                              +

BRIDGET   Yes, of course

             Of course they're going to sell it, I mean

             They haven't done all this, spent all this money,
             just to bring me back from the dead. Have they?

             So it must be

             I must be some kind of prototype, get everything
             working so that they can sell it to people who are

             [*Rich. Scared of dying.*]

                    But you wouldn't

DAVINA   No

BRIDGET   You wouldn't

DAVINA   No, of course not

                    For the first time, DAVINA*'s wondering if she
                    would.*

BRIDGET   I'm sure it would be really

                    I mean really really a lot of / money

DAVINA   Yes

BRIDGET   Although. Your house is very nice.

                              +

PAST BRIDGET   Our kitchen sink leaked

HARRY   Did it?

PAST BRIDGET   Every time we did the washing-up, there'd
                    be this pool of water on the lino

HARRY   What did the kitchen look like?

PAST BRIDGET   White walls. It was

                    That's renting, right? The walls were always

HARRY   And our bedroom?

PAST BRIDGET   The same

HARRY   But we must have decorated

PAST BRIDGET   We put pictures up. Yeah. Those old film
                    stills from the festival

                    I did it for our anniversary, ordered them, got them
                    framed, they were

HARRY   Above the bed

PAST BRIDGET   Yes

HARRY   Tell me more

                              +

DAVINA   What's wrong with having a nice house?

BRIDGET   Nothing. I just meant

DAVINA   What?

+

HARRY   Two weeks ago. The most ordinary – pick the
most ordinary day. And tell me what we did

PAST BRIDGET   Harry

+

BRIDGET   Where is everyone, Davina? Everyone I knew.
They're all dead. All of them.

DAVINA   You want to know what happened?

BRIDGET   Harry wouldn't tell me, not exactly. I mean, he
said it was bad. He said

+

PAST BRIDGET   You made spaghetti Bolognese. You were
meant to go to football. Your five-a-side

+

BRIDGET   No, actually.

What I want to ask is, why are you fine? You and
Harry.

He said you were lucky, but you seem…

Rich.

+

PAST BRIDGET   We stayed in. You watched a documentary,
some wildlife thing, and I was

I had marking to do

+

BRIDGET   So where did the money come from?

DAVINA   Aha.

BRIDGET   You wanted me to ask?

DAVINA   I've been waiting for you to wonder

BRIDGET   Because we were teachers, Harry and I. We were
              just

                              +

PAST BRIDGET   There was a photograph on the landing

                              +

BRIDGET   Is it yours?

DAVINA   God, no

                              +

PAST BRIDGET   There were purple

              Blue

                              +

BRIDGET   So it's Harry's money? But when / did he, how

                              +

PAST BRIDGET   I'm sorry, I don't think I like this, / can we
              please

HARRY   Sorry, Bridget. I wasn't thinking. I was being
              selfish.

PAST BRIDGET   No, it's not –

              I get it, I do

              it's just

              It's too

HARRY   Because I'm so different. It seems too far away

PAST BRIDGET   No

HARRY   Of course. It's been so long

PAST BRIDGET   Well

              Yes. Sometimes, you do seem

HARRY   Different?

          Really?

          I thought

PAST BRIDGET   it's not, / not in a bad way

HARRY   No, no, I just, I thought you said I was the same

          Exactly the same, that's what you said

          BRIDGET *takes over from* PAST BRIDGET.

BRIDGET   Yes. Of course.

          Fifty years, though, Harry.

          Anyone would be different. Wouldn't they?

          BEEP.

6. HUNGER

We're back in the lab.

VICTOR   None of them work.

          None of them work, Mike.

MIKE   Some of these have been very close.

          Closer than I think you realise. Perhaps / we

VICTOR   No, no, I

          I want her again

MIKE   Who?

VICTOR   B389-6.

MIKE   Bridget?

VICTOR   You still have the file, don't you?

MIKE   Well / yeah

VICTOR	So there we go. Easy. / You just
MIKE	But we already brought her back. She's out there, now, walking around
VICTOR	Sure – one version of Bridget. One copy.
	And if you upload her again, there'll be a / new copy
MIKE	Victor
VICTOR	I'm serious. We know she works, we know
MIKE	Yeah but why is she the only one?

Beat.

VICTOR	What?
MIKE	We have spent weeks
	Months
	How is it possible? Think about it. How can she be the / only
VICTOR	I don't know. But if we upload her again, / maybe we can
MIKE	It's you.
	You picked her. I don't know why, but you *made* it work. You made her the first
VICTOR	Bullshit
MIKE	I was there. We rebooted her twenty, thirty times, until it was perfect. Everyone else, you / just give up
VICTOR	Give up?!
MIKE	I'm trying to say that I'm worried / about you
VICTOR	And I am trying to
	End
	Death.
	And you're getting in my way.

MIKE   I'm sorry?

VICTOR   What did you think we were doing here?

MIKE   I thought

            I don't know

            Just life insurance, for rich people. A bit of comfort.

VICTOR   You're a child.

MIKE   You can't actually end

            I mean, it's not something you can just / opt out of

VICTOR   Why not?

            We don't accept smallpox any more, or polio,
            or tetanus. This is progress, Mike. This is
            what it looks like: the end of us accepting the
            unacceptable. Because that's what death is now.
            Unacceptable. The pointless waste of it.

            And I'm sorry if you find my

            Focus

            Alarming

            But there is nothing I wouldn't do to save us all,
            all of us, from the dark.

MIKE   Not with her.

VICTOR   What?

MIKE   Find someone else.

VICTOR   It has to be Bridget.

MIKE   No. She

            She's suffered enough.

VICTOR   What are you talking about? She doesn't even
            remember.

MIKE   But I do.

            I'm not uploading her again, Victor, I refuse.

Did you hear me?

VICTOR *leaves.*

Wait. Where are you going?

Victor.

BRIDGET *is alone onstage.*

She sings 'Glass, Concrete & Stone' by David Byrne.

The CHORUS *enter and sing with her. They sit at the table.*

It is quiet. Then:

HARRY	Davina.
	What am I like?
DAVINA	Sorry?
HARRY	What am I
	If you had to describe me to someone
	What would you say I'm like?
DAVINA	Christ, I don't know, Harry, what's anybody like?
HARRY	Please.
DAVINA	Well, I suppose I'd say that you're
	Clever. You know your own mind. That you're
	Good at making things nice. You want people to be happy, comfortable
HARRY	You mean generous? That I'm generous.
	She laughs.
	Don't.
DAVINA	No. Sorry. I didn't mean to
	Um. You're not ungenerous. You give very thoughtful birthday presents, if / that's what you
HARRY	No, stop. Stop. Please.

DAVINA   I didn't say what you wanted to hear.

HARRY   It's not that. I...

          Beat.

          Where is she?

DAVINA   Bridget? She's not coming to dinner.

HARRY   Oh

DAVINA   She doesn't want to keep coming to / meals, she
          said

HARRY   Right

DAVINA   I think she finds it uncomfortable – watching us
          eat. Not having an appetite.

          Though I can't say I find it all that comfortable
          being watched.

          Beat.

          Harry, do you think it's time for her to go?

HARRY   Go?

DAVINA   Don't look like that. This was only ever supposed
          to be a / temporary

HARRY   You're the one who wanted her to stay. You're the
          one who said we had / a duty, a

DAVINA   Yes, but I didn't mean *forever*. What happened to

          Taking legal advice? Allowing her to

HARRY   No, no

          BRIDGET *is there.* DAVINA *can see her,*
          HARRY *can't.*

DAVINA   Harry

HARRY   No, where would she go, where would she – even
          if we could get everything sorted out, legally,
          which I'm not sure is possible, she'd – do what?
          Live with whom? We're the closest thing to family
          she has left

DAVINA   That doesn't mean she wants to stay indefinitely.

HARRY   How would you know?

BRIDGET   Because I told her.

HARRY   Bridget.

           Beat.

BRIDGET   You said – a lawyer. That you were / going to

HARRY   But that was before

DAVINA   Before what?

HARRY   Before I – we –

           You're being ridiculous

BRIDGET   Am I?

HARRY   Yes, this is / absurd

DAVINA   Okay, do you know what? I might go and clear up, leave you two to talk.

           He barely notices.

HARRY   Okay, thanks.

           Ouch. DAVINA *goes.*

BRIDGET   Harry, I can't stay in this house. It is intolerable.

HARRY   Is this about the meals? Not coming to meals and / not sleeping and

BRIDGET   No

HARRY   You need privacy, I understand. It's not easy. But we can organise

           An annexe, or build some kind of

           Anything, anything you want. Just don't go away again, Bridget, please. Don't take it all with you, / not now

BRIDGET   All what?

HARRY   I

Nothing. I just meant –

I don't even think you really want to go.

BRIDGET   I do.

Harry, I thought I could bear it, but I can't. I

miss you

so much.

HARRY   I'm right here.

BRIDGET   No, I don't mean you, I mean, I miss

Him.

You don't even remember it, you don't remember any of it.

When you talk about who I was –

It's not someone I recognise.

And you are so

completely

different.

Harry, I would rather go away, anywhere, and keep the memory of you intact.

I'm sorry. I am. But please.

Long beat. He's crushed.

HARRY   What are you asking me for? Legal

To be recognised / as

BRIDGET   As a person, I guess, / as myself

HARRY   And take on Edius, one of the richest, most / powerful companies in the

BRIDGET   You're rich. Just call the / most expensive lawyer in

HARRY   That's not fair.

BRIDGET   Harry

HARRY   No, we're comfortable, / but we're not

BRIDGET   I know where the money came from.

            Okay?

            Davina told me.

            Beat.

HARRY   What?

BRIDGET   She told me about the payout from

            After I died

HARRY   It was compensation

BRIDGET   I know

HARRY   It had nothing to do with

            The

            Giving permission. Signing over permission to
            store your

BRIDGET   What?

HARRY   I wasn't paid for that

BRIDGET   I never said you were

HARRY   The money was just compensation.

BRIDGET   Yes, that's what she said

            Sorry, paid / for

HARRY   No, no

BRIDGET   Are you saying they paid you to store my, to use
            my – remains – for / this?

HARRY   No, I'm saying that *didn't* happen

BRIDGET   Jesus

HARRY   I would never, of course I would never, you
            know me

BRIDGET   Right.

Are you sure?

Beat.

HARRY   I'll help you. I'll call the lawyer

BRIDGET   Harry

HARRY   No. Bridget. Look at me. Don't – don't –

BRIDGET   I'm just thinking, I'm not

BEEP.

What's that?

HARRY   The front door. Hold on, I'll

BRIDGET   Get rid of them, please, Harry

VICTOR *is there.*

You.

HARRY   What are you doing here?

VICTOR   I'll be quick. Mr Ingram, I need to talk to you

BRIDGET   What the / hell is

HARRY   Don't worry, I'll handle it

VICTOR   Is there somewhere we can speak privately?

HARRY   It's a bad time.

VICTOR   It's urgent

HARRY   I'm in the middle of a complex, a very
           complicated conversation with my wife

VICTOR   That's / not your wife

BRIDGET   / Harry, I'm not your

HARRY   No, / I just meant

BRIDGET   Davina, Davina is

HARRY   I know

VICTOR   No, sorry, that wasn't what I meant.

Mr Ingram, what I came here to say is

We have reason to believe that this is not your wife. Your late wife.

I mean that this is not Bridget.

Beat.

HARRY   / What?

BRIDGET   No

VICTOR   The technology is still so new. Mistakes can be / made

BRIDGET   'A few / crossed wires'?

VICTOR   And on the day she arrived at your house, she exhibited certain behaviours / which I feel are pertinent to

BRIDGET   / Don't you dare

HARRY   No, go on. What are you

            What behaviours?

VICTOR   Violence. Would you say that was in her nature when she was alive?

HARRY   No. Bridget was

            She was gentle. Kind

BRIDGET   Not always. Harry, not / always

VICTOR   Right – of course she was. Which is why I need to talk to you.

HARRY   Why are you only just, now

VICTOR   Did she tell you what happened, the day she came here?

BRIDGET   Stop

VICTOR   That she held me down and pulled out my eye.

            Beat.

Did she tell you that?

HARRY   Fuck.

What the

Bridget

BRIDGET   I

HARRY   Please

Tell me it isn't true.

A long, horrible beat.

PAST BRIDGET   She can't, of course. Because it is true, and
maybe because she is too busy wondering

Like some part of her is always wondering

If I would have done the same thing.

If I'd been in her position: trapped, scared, feeling
like there was no other option. Could the 'Real
Bridget' really have done what she did?

And she will never, ever, ever know the answer.

She leaves.

HARRY   You.

You

are not

Bridget.

*A rush of noise and activity. People speaking over
each other. Set change.*

BRIDGET   / No

HARRY   Take her away

VICTOR   Thank you, / thank you

BRIDGET   / Harry, please

HARRY   I wanted to believe, but

/ deep down I knew something was wrong. I knew it. Bridget thought the best of me, she knew me, she knew the real me, she would never have

BRIDGET   / you don't have to do this. Call a lawyer, you can

VICTOR   (*Into earpiece.*) Yes please, Mike, let's shut her down for transport

BRIDGET   Wait, wait

The lights go off. Silence.

7. MORE LIFE

In the dim, we see BRIDGET *alone in the lab.* MIKE *beside her.*

She is shaking.

MIKE   What are you doing?

            Are you trying to cry?

            You won't be able to, you know that. You can't. The body can't.

            Beat.

            Bridget, I'm sorry. I tried to stop him, but he was

            Obsessed

            With the thought of getting you back. The real

            'The Real Bridget.' He

            Beat.

            Do you understand what's going to happen tomorrow? Did he explain it to you?

            What did he say?

BRIDGET   Mike, I don't want to do this any more

MIKE   No

BRIDGET   I don't want to be alone like this, I can't bear it

MIKE   No

BRIDGET   Can you turn me off?

            Please.

MIKE   Do you know what tomorrow is?

BRIDGET   Please, Mike

MIKE   Listen, it's important.

            Turning you off is the only threat Vic has, the only
            thing he / can

BRIDGET   I don't care, I don't / care any more

MIKE   No, listen, listen.

            Tomorrow morning, we're taking you upstairs.
            The top floor. We're presenting you, our research,
            to the Board.

            And he wants this for everyone, Bridget. A life
            that is

            Like yours. Without hunger. Without sleep.
            Without death.

            And they'll sell it, and people will buy, and
            everyone
            That's what he said to me
            Everyone
            Is going to want
            What you have.

            Unless…

            He hands her something.

BRIDGET   What's this?

MIKE   I'm giving you the Ops, Bridget

            It's a kind of control panel. For you.

BRIDGET	An off-switch. And then it will just be over, won't it? / It will be
MIKE	Not now.
	Tomorrow. Use it tomorrow.
	Everything you've gone through, you can make it
	For something. Matter. Do you understand what I'm saying?
	Tomorrow. In front of the Board. You can stop them, we can still
	The lights flick on. Bright.
VICTOR	Morning, Bridget.
	Big day.
	Are you ready?
MIKE	Yeah. We're ready, aren't we?
VICTOR	We're about to make history, here, I hope you both realise that.
	No more death.
2	They take her out of the lab, down the winding corridors, towards the lift. Bridget doesn't recognise the way – or only vaguely
4	Half a memory of running, half a memory of Vic's eyeball clenched in her fist
3	Now, she slips a hand into her pocket, grips the Ops, the device Mike gave her. The off-switch
2	She's frightened, but knows it is only animal instinct
4	Misplaced animal instinct in her no-longer-animal body
3	What is there to be frightened of? Just the dark. The not-knowing. On the other hand, if she stays here, she will never really be free

4	And staying will condemn a hundred, or a thousand, or a hundred thousand people to a life like this one.
2	Which is not a life, is it? She has already decided that. It is just an echo.
3	The ripple of a stone dropped into water.
MIKE	Are you ready?
2	They're in the lift
MIKE	Bridget?
2	And it's not a life
BRIDGET	Yes
2	It is not
4	Although it feels like one, sometimes, still.
	Sunrise. Birdsong. Davina's garden. Sometimes even this compromise, this echo, feels like a life
VICTOR	Thank you for coming, all of you
2	The top floor. Suits lining the walls
VICTOR	It has been. The most magnificent. The most exciting
3	Victor talks
4	The suits applaud
BOARD	Thank you
BOARD	Thanks for all your hard work
BOARD	Yes, very excited, of course
3	Bridget's thumb on the button, waiting
2	It is not a life
BOARD	And perhaps she can tell us herself how it feels
BOARD	Yes, Bridget, how does it feel?
2	Not a life

MIKE	Go on, Bridget. Tell them.
	Long beat. Silence.
4	She can't
2	She can
3	She has to
4	No. She can't.
	Beat.
3	*My rage was without bounds; I sprang on the Creature, but he easily eluded me.*
2	*'Be calm, Frankenstein!' he said. 'Have I not suffered enough?*
4	*Life, although it may only be an accumulation of anguish, is dear to me, and I will defend it.'*
BRIDGET	It's been
	So
	Incredible
MIKE	Please
VICTOR	Quiet, Mike
BRIDGET	I died forty-eight years ago, and for decades there was
	Nothing
	And now
2	She lives
BRIDGET	I have it back. All of it.
3	She lives
BRIDGET	Sunrises. Gardens. Coffee. Everything. And it's amazing
2	She lives

5	She lives for / years
6	Years and years and years
5	She lives
4	And lives
2	And goes on living
1	She lives another fourteen years
4	Fourteen years of rain, rivers, burned toast
3	caterpillars
5	snowstorms
3	Before Harry dies.
6	She goes to the funeral. Sits in the front, next to Davina.
1	How retro, Davina says.
5	She says, Tell you what, I won't be having one of these.
3	She's already begun conversations with Edius
2	Already begun to complete the forms.
1	More years pass. Victor ends his human life early, to upload
6	Ready to be free of the tyranny of eating and sleeping and cleaning his infinitely fallible body
4	Mike goes next.
5	He dies young. An accident. Chooses not to upload
1	And soon, there is no one left who is quite as they were.
	Who remembers Bridget quite as she was.
	Beat.
4	Never mind. She goes on. Living is what she does

2	Whole autumns watching a hedgerow die back
3	Whole springs watching birds nest in a treetop
1	She's not human any more, whatever that was – but who is, these days?
6	And still they want
ALL	More
2	All of them, still wanting
ALL	More
5	Because a half-life is better than no life at all. Of course it is, look at this place, it's magnificent
4	And the years pass
ALL	(*Jumbled.*) and pass and pass and pass and pass and pass
6	Until Bridget stands
	Hundreds?
3	It could be hundreds
1	It could be more. Much more.
2	Let's say hundreds, are we happy with that?
5	Hundreds of years after her human death, Bridget stands beside the women who are weeping.
4	They pull their clothes
3	They wear black
2	And white
1	And there are candles
6	And ash
ALL	A funeral
1	While Bridget watches.
3	It is her six-hundred-and-seventy-third funeral.

2	Davina was wrong. They didn't go out of style. But they didn't stay quite the same, either.
4	There is ash, and sobbing, and prayer in a language that did not exist when the person who used to be Bridget was born.
2	Does she remember how it felt to stand at Harry's grave?
5	It's been a long time. A very, very, very long time. Does she even remember who Harry was?
6	Does she remember her childhood?
5	Does she remember she had a sister?
6	Does she remember how scared she was, the whole year she was eleven, that her sister was going to die?
3	Does she remember how it felt, in 2074, to hear that she actually had?
1	Bridget's travelled further than anyone could have imagined. And, now, here she is: a funeral for the last
2	The last
5	The last

Zing! Aldini's generator cuts out. Blackout. Silence.

Then: a light on PAST BRIDGET*'s face.*

Like the light from a phone in the dark.

1	A woman lies awake in the middle of the night.
4	It's cold, the winter of 2025, cold and wet, and her husband is sleeping beside her.
3	He always sleeps annoyingly well.
5	She has three hundred and eighty days left to live.
4	Three hundred and eighty days, or several hundred

years, depending how you look at it.

Beat.

6	Bridget has a bad habit on nights like this, nights when sleep doesn't come:
4	Scrolling. She reads on her phone.
5	Yes, the blue light will make the insomnia worse, yes, she knows this
1	And it drives Harry mad, but who cares. He's asleep
3	Annoyingly very annoyingly deeply asleep.

Beat.

6	Sometimes she reads the news. The love affairs of celebrities, the more boring the better. Rich people's kitchens being done up
5	anything to put her to sleep
2	but tonight, she is doomscrolling: link to link to link, and then a rabbit hole, reading about one of the futures
6	From where she sits, there are so many possible futures
4	Catastrophe. The waters rising
3	Medical miracles
5	Flying cars.
1	This one is a future without death.
4	It's being made with billions and billions and billions of dollars, on the other side of the world, for men who think that they should never have to die.

HARRY   Bridget, please. The light's waking me up.

BRIDGET(S)   Sorry.

6	Bridget shuts her phone off, puts it beneath her

	pillow, goes back to lying in the dark
2	Back to what she was thinking before:
5	things she has to do tomorrow. Change the bedsheets. Take the bins down. Email Val
1	But not just that. She thinks about the things she was reading.
6	Her brain pings with words like *cryogenics*. Heavy, unreal words, straight out of a film
3	Sci-fi. Or maybe horror.
1	And as she lies in the dark beside her husband
2	Who is very warm
5	As she lies there, listening to his breathing
6	Waiting for sleep to claim her
3	She thinks
4	Thank god none of that will ever happen.

Darkness.

End.

A Nick Hern Book

More Life first published in Great Britain in 2025 as a paperback original by Nick Hern Books Limited, The Glasshouse, 49a Goldhawk Road, London W12 8QP, in association with Kandinsky Theatre Company and the Royal Court Theatre, London

Cover image: Guy Sanders at Keeper Studio

Designed and typeset by Nick Hern Books, London
Printed in the UK by Mimeo Ltd, Huntingdon, Cambridgeshire PE29 6XX

A CIP catalogue record for this book is available from the British Library

ISBN   978 1 83904 423 6

Woodland
CARBON
www.woodlandcarbon.co.uk
NICK HERN BOOKS
Printed on Carbon Captured paper

www.nickhernbooks.co.uk/environmental-policy

Nick Hern Books' authorised representative in the EU is
Easy Access System Europe – Mustamäe tee 50, 10621 Tallinn, Estonia
email gpsr.requests@easproject.com